Monad

Other Microsoft Windows resources from O'Reilly

Related titles   Active Directory
        Cookbook™
    Active Directory
    Windows Server 2003
        Network
        Administration

    Windows Server 2003
        Security Cookbook™
    Windows Server
        Cookbook™
    Learning Windows
        Server 2003

Windows Books Resource Center   *windows.oreilly.com* is a complete catalog of O'Reilly's Windows and Office books, including sample chapters and code examples.

oreillynet.com is the essential portal for developers interested in open and emerging technologies, including new platforms, programming languages, and operating systems.

Conferences   O'Reilly brings diverse innovators together to nurture the ideas that spark revolutionary industries. We specialize in documenting the latest tools and systems, translating the innovator's knowledge into useful skills for those in the trenches. Visit *conferences.oreilly.com* for our upcoming events.

Safari Bookshelf (*safari.oreilly.com*) is the premier online reference library for programmers and IT professionals. Conduct searches across more than 1,000 books. Subscribers can zero in on answers to time-critical questions in a matter of seconds. Read the books on your Bookshelf from cover to cover or simply flip to the page you need. Try it today for free.

Monad

Andy Oakley

Beijing · Cambridge · Farnham · Köln · Sebastopol · Tokyo

Monad

by Andy Oakley

Copyright © 2006 O'Reilly Media, Inc. All rights reserved.
Printed in the United States of America.

Published by O'Reilly Media, Inc., 1005 Gravenstein Highway North, Sebastopol, CA 95472.

O'Reilly books may be purchased for educational, business, or sales promotional use. Online editions are also available for most titles (*safari.oreilly.com*). For more information, contact our corporate/institutional sales department: (800) 998-9938 or *corporate@oreilly.com*.

Editors:	John Osborn and Robbie Allen
Production Editor:	Marlowe Shaeffer
Cover Designer:	Karen Montgomery
Interior Designer:	David Futato

Printing History:

December 2005:	First Edition.

ISBN: 978-0-596-10009-4

Table of Contents

Foreword

Monad is a next generation shell or command interpreter that embraces traditional shell concepts by providing interactive and simple scripting experiences. However, Monad breaks new ground by leveraging the power of objects, providing a full-featured language with native support for rich data types, and refactoring the shell, commands, and utilities. The result is a shell that supports a wide range of users from interactive command-line users to the most sophisticated scripters.

I started the Monad project with the intention of rewriting WMIC, the command-line interface to Windows Management Infrastructure, in C# (WMI is one of the primary APIs used to manage Windows). WMIC proved to be a very successful endeavor; it has a common command-line engine to do parsing, error handling, and object manipulation; and it uses small amounts of metadata to drive the engine to manipulate WMI objects. This architecture provides some important economic incentives:

- Every improvement made to the engine benefits every command, providing an economic incentive to improve the engine.
- Users have common syntaxes and semantics to all commands, providing an economic incentive to learn how to use the tool.
- Only a small amount of metadata is required to create commands, providing an economic incentive to generate commands

While the power of WMIC is awesome, it has a syntax that many find awkward. It is completely dependent on WMI coverage, which is good for Windows but troublesome for third parties. While developing the architecture, Bill Gates beat me up regularly because our management technologies did not provide adequate support for .NET programs. I decided it was time to find out what had him so excited.

I learned .NET by rewriting WMIC in C#, fixing up its syntax, and adding support for XML. During the process, I found .NET Reflection. I was delighted to discover that it provided about 70 percent of what was needed from WMI (e.g., the ability to ask any object to state its properties/methods, get the property values, and invoke the methods). At that point, I realized that the architectural power of WMIC could be applied to any .NET object, and that's when things took off.

We formed a team and fleshed out all of the details. We transformed the core concepts into a full-fledged automation environment that included an interactive shell, a powerful scripting language, a rich set of utility functions, a set of commands, and an SDK. We envisioned a program that would make it as easy to interact with data stores as it is to interact with the filesystem. Our vision was to produce something that would be as interactive and composable as KSH or BASH, as programmatic as Perl or Python, as production-oriented as AS400 CL or VMS DCL, and as embeddable as TCL or WSH.

Most of the people on the team have extensive experience working with COM and Unix. COM scripting is powerful, but it requires you to work at a programmer's level of abstraction. The Unix composition model is also powerful, but it provides an escape valve that relieves you of any pressure you might feel to go back and refactor the tools. When SH didn't support what you needed to do, you just wrote a new tool such as AWK; and when AWK didn't meet your needs, you had to write yet another tool. Each of these tools required a new learning curve (and sometimes a new set of books). While the Monad team has enormous respect for these programs, we knew we had some improvements to contribute.

Jim Truher, our shell program manager (PM), is experienced in working with Unix scripting. His input was invaluable in preserving the essential semantics of the Unix model, while reframing them in a way that led to a more consistent syntax and improved user experience. Bruce Payette, our development lead, is a walking encyclopedia of languages and was able to educate us about the outcome of just about every good, bad, and wacky idea that has ever been tried out in a language. Kenneth Hansen, our SDK PM, has an extensive background working with provisioning systems. He crafted a namespace model that allows you to interact with all the data stores (e.g., the Registry, the Certificate store, and—in the future—Active Directory, SQL, etc.) the same way you interact with the filesystem. In addition to Unix and system/network management, I have developed and used VMS systems, the operating system of the DEC VAX minicomputers. Also, I am a big fan of the IBM AS400 and its command language (CL). Both of these environments have a strong focus on production qualities and naming/syntactic consistency.

Together, we felt that it was time to step back and perform a "grand refactoring" among the shell, the utilities, the language, and the commands. Our goal was to incorporate the best of these environments into a single cohesive program.

The result is Monad. Whether you are looking for a better Windows command-line shell, a simple environment to crank out ad hoc scripts, or a hardcore scripting language to generate and publish sophisticated production scripts, Monad should meet all of your needs. We think you'll like it.

—Jeffrey P. Snover
Monad Architect

Preface

Monad is the code name for the new interactive command-line and task-based scripting technology in Windows. Also known as MSH, it is the next generation of the Windows command shell that provides a new way of thinking about a wide range of administrative tasks. At last, to the relief of administrators and power users everywhere, the command line is truly becoming a first-class citizen in the world of Windows system management.

I wrote *Monad* to give you a first look at the MSH command shell, and to get you to start using it as quickly as possible. You won't find this book to be the comprehensive tutorial or dry reference manual that typically accompanies a new product like MSH; rather, it's an exciting hands-on tour of the most useful new capabilities that MSH brings to the table.

Who This Book Is For

From administrators to developers to power users, MSH has something for everyone. If you're someone who finds your fingers habitually drifting toward the c-m-d keys, who knows all of the switches to most command-line tools, or who spends time authoring batch files to solve new challenges, this book is definitely for you.

MSH has wide appeal. If you have a background in using other shells (on Unix like platforms, for example), keep reading: console-based command-line interaction in Windows has come a long way and there's plenty of new stuff to see. Even if you're just intrigued by this new technology, the content in this book doesn't assume any specialized domain knowledge; you may find your toolbox just gained another tool.

How This Book Is Organized

Monad consists of seven chapters and two appendixes. Each chapter has a series of hands-on labs that show you how to use MSH to complete a particular task. Some labs familiarize you with key concepts, such as how to use the pipeline, while others show you how to perform common tasks, such as displaying the contents of a registry hive. Each lab introduces a task, shows you how to do it, and explains what happens when MSH runs the command or script used in the lab. In addition, each lab tries to answer common "What If..." questions and offers suggestions for further reading.

Chapter 1, *Introducing MSH*
> Covers the basics, such as downloading and installing the shell itself, using the MSH noun-verb syntax, passing information via a pipeline, and displaying data in the console.

Chapter 2, *Customizing MSH*
> Moves into the command shell usage, including writing and running scripts, time-saving techniques, and personalizing the default MSH environment.

Chapter 3, *Scripting MSH*
> Looks at the relationship with the .NET Framework, and contains the details of the scripting language with its objects, variables, script flow techniques, and functions.

Chapter 4, *Managing MSH Scope and State*
> Dives into some of the deeper aspects of the scripting language, such as variable scope, as well as topics in string manipulation and error handling.

Chapter 5, *Adding to the MSH Toolkit*
> Introduces a handful of indispensable commands that come standard, and teaches how to load and save data, as well as how to use the .NET Framework and Component Object Model (COM) extension points.

Chapter 6, *Working with Operating System Components*
> Covers interaction with the Windows infrastructure, including the event log, system services, and WMI.

Chapter 7, *Putting MSH to Work*
> Shows some practical applied uses of the shell, including interoperability with *cmd.exe*-based tools, batch file migration, and a library of useful MSH hacks.

Appendix A, *Syntax and Grammar*
> Provides a quick reference guide to the language of the shell, broken out by commands, data types, variables, and language constructs.

Appendix B, *Standard Cmdlets, Functions, and Aliases*
  Lists the built-in commands with a brief description of each.

What You Need to Use This Book

To get the most out of this book, you need a system running one of the following Microsoft Windows platforms:

- Microsoft Windows XP SP2
- Microsoft Windows Server 2003 SP1
- Microsoft Windows Vista (formerly known as Longhorn)

You'll also need a running copy of MSH. Although the examples stand on their own, there is much to be learned by trying them out, tweaking them, and extending them for other purposes. For detailed instructions on how to download and install the command shell, see "Get MSH" in Chapter 1.

Programming or scripting skills are not a prerequisite to enjoying this book. I'm confident you'll find that most of the content of *Monad* is relevant to system administrators, developers, and power users alike.

Conventions Used in This Book

The following typographical conventions are used in this book:

Plain text
  Indicates menu titles, menu options, menu buttons, and keyboard accelerators (such as Alt and Ctrl).

Italic
  Indicates new terms, URLs, email addresses, filenames, file extensions, pathnames, directories, and Unix utilities.

Constant width
  Indicates commands, options, switches, variables, attributes, keys, functions, types, classes, namespaces, methods, modules, properties, parameters, values, objects, events, event handlers, XML tags, HTML tags, macros, the contents of files, or the output from commands.

Constant width bold
  Shows commands or other text that should be typed literally by the user.

Constant width italic
  Shows text that should be replaced with user-supplied values.

This icon signifies a tip, suggestion, or general note.

 This icon indicates a warning or caution.

Using Code Examples

This book is here to help you get your job done. In general, you may use the code in this book in your programs and documentation. You do not need to contact us for permission unless you're reproducing a significant portion of the code. For example, writing a program that uses several chunks of code from this book does not require permission. Selling or distributing a CD-ROM of examples from O'Reilly books *does* require permission. Answering a question by citing this book and quoting example code does not require permission. Incorporating a significant amount of example code from this book into your product's documentation *does* require permission.

We appreciate, but do not require, attribution. An attribution usually includes the title, author, publisher, and ISBN. For example: "*Monad* by Andy Oakley. Copyright 2006 O'Reilly Media, Inc., 0-596-10009-4"

If you feel your use of code examples falls outside fair use or the permission given above, feel free to contact us at *permissions@oreilly.com*.

How to Contact Us

Please address comments and questions concerning this book to the publisher:

> O'Reilly Media, Inc.
> 1005 Gravenstein Highway North
> Sebastopol, CA 95472
> (800) 998-9938 (in the U.S. or Canada)
> (707) 829-0515 (international or local)
> (707) 829-0104 (fax)

We have a web page for this book, where we list errata, examples, and any additional information. You can access this page at:

> *http://www.oreilly.com/catalog/msh*

To comment or ask technical questions about this book, send email to:

bookquestions@oreilly.com

For more information about our books, conferences, Resource Centers, and the O'Reilly Network, see our web site at:

http://www.oreilly.com

Safari® Enabled

 When you see a Safari® Enabled icon on the cover of your favorite technology book, that means the book is available online through the O'Reilly Network Safari Bookshelf.

Safari offers a solution that's better than e-books. It's a virtual library that lets you easily search thousands of top tech books, cut and paste code samples, download chapters, and find quick answers when you need the most accurate, current information. Try it for free at *http://safari.oreilly.com*.

Acknowledgments

I'd like to thank the reviewers—Robbie Allen, Alex Angelopoulos, Adam Barr, Leonard Chung, Lee Holmes, and Jon Newman—for their valuable feedback during the writing process. I'd also like to thank John Osborn of O'Reilly for his guidance and patience with this book. Special thanks also go to Chris Sells for opening the door to this opportunity.

None of this would have been possible without the hard work of the people of the Monad team at Microsoft who have done a fantastic job of building a great tool.

Finally, I'd like to thank Katie Shangraw for her support and all of my friends and family who have, at times, been left wondering "Where is Andy?" during the writing of this book.

## CHAPTER 1

Introducing MSH

Monad, also known more formally as the MSH Command Shell, is a next generation Windows command shell. Built on top of the .NET Framework, MSH provides a powerful infrastructure for the automation of a wide range of administrative tasks. At last, the command line is a first-class citizen in the world of Windows system management.

It would be unfair to characterize MSH as simply an evolution of the *cmd.exe* shell, a system whose roots reach back to the days of MS-DOS and before. Indeed, although the standard "host" of MSH is a console application, MSH is designed so that it can be used in other contexts, such as the MMC (Microsoft Management Console). This new shell is built from the ground up with a focus on structured data and today's administrative challenges.

The *pipeline*, a mechanism for passing data between different functional units, has long been a feature of many shells, including *cmd.exe*. MSH goes beyond the traditional notion of using text to pass data between the different stages of the pipeline and all of the "prayer-based parsing" that goes with it by allowing the transfer of structured data in the form of .NET objects between the pipeline elements. This self-describing information can be used at any point in a complex sequence and allows any process to operate on data in an intelligent fashion, even pipeline elements that have never seen a given type of data before.

MSH also uses a *provider model* so that the many types of hierarchical data stores used with Windows systems can be accessed through a single consistent set of commands. In MSH, the mechanism for retrieving folders, files, content, and the current location applies not only to filesystems but also to other stores, such as the registry.

Repeatability and consistency are the two words that capture some of the real value of using MSH. Administering a single machine today is a simple task; Windows offers a well-organized graphical interface for settings and configuration, and Terminal Services makes it easy to effect changes on a server located on the other side of the world. Unfortunately, in simple terms, this model doesn't scale well at all; it takes twice as long to manage 2 machines and 10 times as long for 10. Fortunately, there are management tools such as Systems Management Server (SMS) that ease this burden across the enterprise. Also, technologies such as WSH (Windows Scripting Host) and Perl can be used to automate repetitive tasks. By offering a scriptable language, MSH offers yet another alternative to the manual click-by-click sequence where a one-time investment in authoring a configuration script enables quick replay on a potentially large number of machines with predictable results. Add this all up, and there's a lot of time to be saved.

Let's take a moment to dispel a few rumors about MSH. The new shell is not a programming language to be compared with C#, C++, or VB.NET, yet it does offer a powerful scripting language. Although MSH relies heavily on the .NET Framework, it is first and foremost an administrative tool. As we'll see, MSH is a hybrid, taking the idea of a command shell and combining it with a rich scripting language to form something altogether more useful. MSH isn't going to replace everything in a system manager's toolbox either; in fact, think of MSH as a conduit that provides easy access to preexisting components whether they are exposed through the .NET Framework, COM objects, or some other mechanism. *cmd.exe* isn't going away either; MSH even offers support for other command-line utilities that process text. The existing command-line toolset will continue to live, and investments made in console-based applications remain valuable. Finally, MSH is not positioned to encroach on the realm of software builds. While it offers a number of features useful in a large build environment, it's a complement to NMAKE, MSBuild, or Visual Studio Team System, rather than a drop-in replacement for them.

These are just a few of the features of MSH that are causing Windows system administrators to take notice. As a shell, it brings together some powerful concepts by leveraging the .NET Framework and COM, and by allowing existing tools to be reused rather than reinvented. As we'll soon see, a tool like this has a very wide range of uses.

Get MSH

MSH is supported on a number of currently available Microsoft operating systems. To use MSH, you'll need to be running on one of the following platforms:

- Microsoft Windows XP SP2
- Microsoft Windows Server 2003 SP1
- Microsoft Windows Vista (formerly Windows Code Name "Longhorn")

In addition to a supported operating system, MSH requires the .NET Framework 2.0 redistributable, SDK, or Visual Studio 2005.

Downloading MSH

Everything needed to get up and running can be downloaded from the Web. Follow these installation steps and you'll be ready to go:

1. Download and install the .NET Framework 2.0 Redistributable from *http://msdn.microsoft.com/netframework/downloads/updates/default.aspx*. Several versions are available for different machine architectures (32-bit and 64-bit); pick the one suitable for your machine.

2. Go to *http://download.microsoft.com* and search for "Monad". Download and install the latest release.

That's it. Let's get started!

Get to Know Verb-Noun Syntax and Cmdlets

We'll begin by getting the shell up and running so that we can start to put MSH through its paces. This section will focus on the time-honored task of inspecting the process list to see what's currently running on a system. There are some MSH features that may not be immediately familiar to those in other command shells—in particular, the strict command syntax—but we'll also look at a few of the obvious differences and see how they're really nothing to fear.

These basics show you how to start using the shell, and they provide the foundation for the rest of the examples we'll cover.

How Do I Do That?

Most MSH commands are identified by a pair of words, one verb and one noun, separated by a hyphen. The verb describes the action (such as get or set) while the noun represents the target of the action in singular form (such as process or location). There is a standard list of verbs that covers the majority of tasks (including get, set, add, and remove). Although the number of these verbs may seem excessively large, consistent naming does make learning and using MSH easier in the long run.

There's Nothing Like Experience

The best way to learn more about MSH is to start using it. Begin with simple tasks—such as viewing the task list and folder structure—and then start experimenting. Be careful, though, because some cmdlets can have significant impact. For example, if you ask MSH to delete all of your files, it will do so without remorse. As we'll see in Chapter 2, adding the -WhatIf command-line option will perform a "dry run" in which MSH tells you what it would do without really doing it.

Let's begin by starting the shell. From the Start menu, select Run and type **MSH**. You'll see a console window open up with a small introduction:

```
Microsoft Command Shell
Copyright (C) 2005 Microsoft Corporation. All rights reserved.

MSH D:\MshScripts>
```

MSH is waiting for its first command. The MSH shell is in interactive mode with the current directory set to *D:\MshScripts*. We'll look at the different modes of operation in more detail later on. For now, the shell will execute commands line-by-line as they are entered.

Running a first command

We'll use the get-process cmdlet to generate a list of currently active processes within the system:

```
MSH D:\MshScripts> get-process

Handles  NPM(K)    PM(K)      WS(K) VS(M)   CPU(s)     Id ProcessName
-------  ------    -----      ----- -----   ------     -- -----------
    119       6      996       3336    31     0.22   1844 alg
    602      12    10408      15816    64    18.96   1656 CcmExec
    409       5     1648       3364    22    16.23    464 csrss
    273      11     7376      12696    55   340.16    212 explorer
      0       0        0         16     0             0 Idle
    146      11     3532       7284    61     2.90   1264 InoRpc
    110       5    11136      12404    60     9.33   1316 InoRT
    107       5     2820       6244    53     4.22   1332 InoTask
    405      10     4404        528    41    11.66    544 lsass
    290      12    33948      32208   175    14.90   3088 msh
    ...
```

You can use a command line or argument to reduce the number of processes get-process returns. Given something to match against, get-process will compare the process name of each process, only allowing matching ones to be displayed. Let's take a look at all processes beginning with the letter "r" or "s":

```
MSH D:\MshScripts> get-process [rs]*

Handles  NPM(K)    PM(K)      WS(K) VS(M)   CPU(s)     Id ProcessName
-------  ------    -----      ----- -----   ------     -- -----------
     96       4     1772       4972    43    54.60   1200 Realmon
    260       6     1260       2840    24    13.38    532 services
     21       1      168        368     4     0.57    308 smss
     96       4     2428       3208    26     0.32   1088 spoolsv
    207       6     2056       4312    35     4.41    940 svchost
    251      13     1472       3968    34     8.20    756 svchost
   1665      50    14648      22040    98    44.27    824 svchost
    183       5     2280       4440    57     0.64    720 svchost
     85       4     1036       2968    28     2.44    896 svchost
    284       0        0        216     2    64.20      4 System
```

get-process will accept another parameter called Exclude. This is used to filter certain processes from the results list. This time, we'll find all processes starting with the letter "w," except those that start with the three letters "win":

```
MSH D:\MshScripts> get-process w* -Exclude win*

Handles  NPM(K)    PM(K)      WS(K) VS(M)   CPU(s)     Id ProcessName
-------  ------    -----      ----- -----   ------     -- -----------
    125       4     1300       3624    23     0.82    320 wmiprvse
    137       4     3388       4156    25     1.36   1920 wmiprvse
    221       7     6352       7868    65     2.60   1708 wuauclt
```

What Just Happened?

Let's take a step back and look at what we've just witnessed. To better understand how get-process works, let's start from the top.

What is a cmdlet?

Cmdlets (pronounced "command-lets") are one of the fundamental parts of the functionality of MSH. Cmdlets range from the very simple to the very complex, but all are designed to do a single task and to do it well. MSH provides a framework within which these cmdlets can be run, effectively providing the plumbing for passing information between different pipeline elements. Cmdlets are not designed to be monolithic giants that completely solve any given problem; instead, their power derives from composition— their use in concert with other cmdlets. A well-designed cmdlet focuses on doing one job in a clear and predictable manner. We'll be talking a lot more about cmdlets and composition going forward.

A cmdlet is implemented as a managed class (built on the .NET Framework) that implements a well-defined set of methods to process data.

Why the verb-noun model?

Although the verb-noun syntax may seem slightly foreign or even cumbersome, there are rewards in its consistency. Because we already know how to list active processes with the get-process command, it's only a small jump to manipulate processes by using other verbs, for example stop-process and new-process. The symmetry in cmdlet naming helps to group commands based on either task or target, which makes it easy to use other related cmdlets by picking one of the set of common verbs. It's worth noting that the verb-noun requirement applies only to cmdlets; as we meet other MSH concepts such as functions, scripts, and aliases, we'll see that they are not subject to the same strict syntax.

If you're concerned that get-process requires more keystrokes than tasklist (its nearest *cmd.exe* equivalent), or that get-childitem is significantly longer than dir, rest assured that there are shortcuts in the form of command aliases. We look into aliases in more detail in Chapter 2. For now, we'll continue to use the long form as it generally improves the readability of scripts.

 All nouns have a default verb, get, which is assumed if no verb is given. In other words, the command process will behave in exactly the same manner as get-process.

What About...

In itself, generating a process list isn't rocket science. tlist.exe, part of the Windows Resource Kit, has been offering this functionality for years. However, the MSH version is going to enable us to do a lot more. In the next few examples, we'll see how this cmdlet can be combined with others to offer some flexible process list reporting.

We'll look at wildcards in Chapter 4, but it is worth mentioning now that the [rs]* and win* style syntax used here isn't restricted to the get-process cmdlet. In fact, it is actually MSH that interprets the command-line parameters (not the cmdlets), and the shell extends this kind of wildcard support and parsing consistency throughout.

Where Can I Learn More?

The get-help cmdlet is the portal into the built-in help system for MSH. By simply giving it a cmdlet name, a help page covering the syntax and usage will be shown:

```
MSH D:\MshScripts> get-help get-process

NAME
    get-process

SYNOPSIS
    Gets a list of processes on a machine.

DETAILED DESCRIPTION
    The get-process Cmdlet gets a list of the process running on a machine
    and displays it to the console along with the process properties.

    This command also supports the ubiquitous parameters:
    -Debug (-db), -ErrorAction (-ea), -ErrorVariable (-ev)
    -OutBuffer (-ob), -OutVariable (-ov), and -Verbose (-vb)

SYNTAX
    get-process [-ProcessName] [processName] [-Id processId]
    ...
```

Calling get-help without any parameters generates an overview of the available help topics. Specific help information is available by supplying a topic or cmdlet name.

The get-command cmdlet provides a mechanism for listing all cmdlets registered with the shell, including their signature, parameter list, and description.

Since we're on the quick tour, let's take a look at one of the new aspects of MSH: the ability to treat arbitrary data stores like regular filesystems by way of a provider model.

Access the Registry Like a Filesystem

Historically, command-line shells have been intimately tied to the filesystem. With a well-defined hierarchical structure, commands are provided to move up, down, and around; work on items at some location within; or even to extend or contract the structure. Many years have shown a hierarchy is an effective representation of a data store, even if it does introduce a few problems—for example when trying to manipulate a set of items scattered in different locations throughout the tree.

Of course, it hasn't always been possible to look at a filesystem in the single consolidated manner that we enjoy today. Even with the variety of stores and protocols now in use—from FAT, NTFS, and CIFS to ISO9660—modern operating systems abstract the differences away from us, leaving a single, simple view of hierarchical folders and files. MSH takes this concept a step further and embraces other hierarchical data stores, such as the registry, to enable us to navigate around them and act within them as if they were a simple folder structure on disk. As we're about to see, this makes many tasks much easier.

In MSH, a *provider* forms the abstraction layer that exposes a hierarchical store to the shell as another drive. In addition to the familiar *A*, *C*, and *D* drives, you can now see drives representing environment variables, MSH functions, shortcuts to *My Documents*, and parts of the registry. This list isn't fixed and drives can be added, each backed by a different provider.

Let's take a look at the simple example of Windows Notepad and how to change its configuration via the registry.

I Thought the Registry Was a Move Away from the Filesystem...

The MSH provider model isn't a throwback to the days of filesystem-based configuration. Instead, making the store look like a regular disk drive allows us to use a single toolset to manipulate a wide range of information stored in disparate locations.

Just think: a script designed to walk through a folder structure doing a global search and replace can now do exactly the same via the registry with few, if any, changes.

How Do I Do That?

The registry is divided into five primary divisions known as *hives*, two of which we'll look at here. HKEY_LOCAL_MACHINE (often abbreviated to HKLM) stores system-wide settings shared by all users of the machine. HKEY_CURRENT_USER (HKCU) contains the current user's settings and user-specific information.

When it starts, MSH installs two additional drives (named hkcu: and hklm:) that map to these two hives. You can start browsing around them right away:

```
MSH D:\MshScripts> cd hkcu:
MSH D:\MshScripts> dir

SKC  VC ChildName                   Property
---  -- ---------                   --------
  2   0 AppEvents                   {}
  0  31 Console                     {ColorTable00, ColorTable01,
                                     ColorTab...
 23   1 Control Panel               {Opened}
  0   3 Environment                 {MSHCOMMANDPATH, TEMP, TMP}
  1   6 Identities                  {Identity Ordinal, Migrated5, Last
                                     Us...
  2   0 Keyboard Layout             {}
  0   0 Network                     {}
  1   0 Printers                    {}
  5   0 Software                    {}
  0   0 UNICODE Program Groups      {}
  0   1 SessionInformation          {ProgramCount}
  0   7 Volatile Environment        {LOGONSERVER, CLIENTNAME,
                                     SESSIONNAME...
```

For comparison, it's easy to see the relationship between this output and the tree structure shown in the Registry Editor tool (*regedit.exe*), as displayed in Figure 1-1.

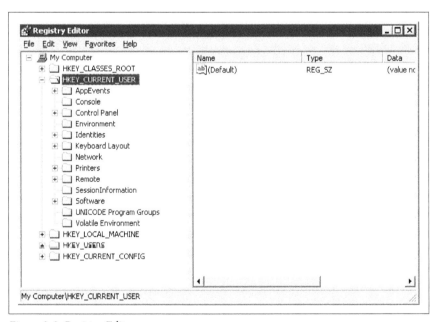

Figure 1-1. Registry Editor

Notepad stores its per-user settings in the HKCU hive under the *Software* *Microsoft* path. We can navigate to that path with a simple cd and use the get-property cmdlet to view its content:

```
MSH D:\MshScripts> cd hkcu:\Software\Microsoft\Notepad
MSH D:\MshScripts> get-property .

lfEscapement          : 0
lfOrientation         : 0
lfWeight              : 400
lfItalic              : 0
lfUnderline           : 0
lfStrikeOut           : 0
lfCharSet             : 0
lfOutPrecision        : 1
lfClipPrecision       : 2
lfQuality             : 2
lfPitchAndFamily      : 49
iPointSize            : 100
fWrap                 : 0
StatusBar             : 0
fSaveWindowPositions  : 0
lfFaceName            : Lucida Console
szHeader              : &f
szTrailer             : Page &p
iMarginTop            : 1000
iMarginBottom         : 1000
iMarginLeft           : 750
iMarginRight          : 750
fMLE_is_broken        : 0
iWindowPosX           : 88
iWindowPosY           : 88
iWindowPosDX          : 600
iWindowPosDY          : 411
```

Return to REGEDIT for a moment and it's easy to see that this output directly corresponds to the content of the righthand pane when the Notepad node is selected. Notepad uses the lfFaceName key to store the font used for displaying content. We'll use the set-property cmdlet (notice we're using the same noun, just a different verb) to change this value to Verdana:

```
MSH D:\MshScripts> set-property . -property lfFaceName -value "Verdana"
```

Now when we start Notepad, it'll load the new setting from the registry for the content area and display it in a different font, as seen in Figure 1-2.

What About…

…Using this approach to configure any application? It depends. Applications can store configuration settings in many places, such as XML files, INI files, Active Directory, and the registry. Each application may pick a different

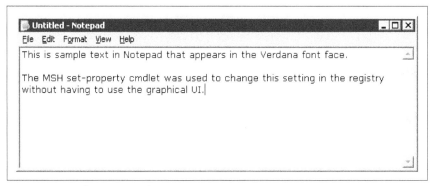

Figure 1-2. Windows Notepad

approach that works well for its specific scenario, but this doesn't guarantee any consistency. Even applications that don't wholly rely on the registry don't follow one single format or naming convention in use, although typically you'll find settings under *\Software\[Vendor name]\[Application name]*. You can use the graphical REGEDIT tool or the commands we've seen here to explore the registry further.

Although we've only looked at the registry provider in this section, the same process works for other stores with providers offered by the shell.

At this point, it's fair to ask, "Aren't there other tools for this?" and "What about Group Policy and SMS?" Indeed, there are many tools on the Windows platform for application management that excel at their tasks. MSH isn't designed to replace those; instead, MSH levels the field, allowing immediate interactive exploration of the system. Group Policy and SMS are invaluable in large automated deployments, and MSH can be considered a complement for day-to-day administration. Use MSH if it makes sense for a task, but remember it supports, rather than replaces, the suite of management tools available today.

Where Can I Learn More?

The Windows registry is described in more detail at *http://support.microsoft.com/default.aspx?scid=kb;EN-US;256986*. As the article notes, changing values in the registry is not a subject to be taken lightly. Be sure you know which values you're changing and the effect they'll have before making any changes to production machines.

The get-provider cmdlet lists the providers currently registered with MSH, along with the drives that use them. Similarly, get-drive will list all physical drives (hard disks, removable media), as well as those relying on provider-based systems.

Moving on, it's time to take a look at some of the fundamental changes to the pipeline in MSH.

Create a Pipeline to Pass Information

The *cmd.exe* command shell has always supported the idea of redirecting the output of a process to a different location. The vertical bar, or pipe symbol (|), is used to create this pipeline. When present, it instructs the shell to redirect the output of one command to the input stream of another, effectively chaining the commands together. For example, while the command type win.ini | more is a familiar way of paging through a long text file, what's really happening is that the output of the type command, which lists the contents of a file in its entirety, is being piped to the more command, which knows how big the screen is and how to pause when it's full.

The pipeline is not a new concept and is the glue that most command shells use for passing data between different processes. However, MSH takes the concept one step further. Instead of passing simple text streams between different steps (the method used by almost all command shells today), for communication between MSH cmdlets and scripts, strongly typed objects are used to carry both the information and its structure.

Passing strongly typed data has some significant advantages. Flat text files are rarely the best way to represent structured data as there is only so much information that can be captured in a line-to-line text listing. Historically, when information is transferred between two processes in textual format, there will be some mutually agreed upon encoding—maybe the generator will always output information in some sequence that the receiver must then parse to recreate the structure for processing. Authors must either add complexity to their tool by generating both human-readable and machine-readable output, or they end up forcing the script writer to use a parsing tool such as AWK to extract meaning from the textual output. Such parsers can be difficult to write, are prone to failure with minor tool changes, and cannot always handle international characters. Clearly, this tightly binds the two tools together, requiring code in both to handle the interchange. This is often so restrictive that it limits the tools so that they cannot be used for any other purpose. With MSH passing structured data instead of text, much of this encoding and decoding effort disappears and arbitrary pipelines become a reality.

The pipeline empowers MSH through composition. *Composition*, in this sense, refers to the way in which we can combine small functional units together, creating something altogether more useful. As we discussed earlier, cmdlets are designed to do a simple task well—for example, listing processes, sorting, and filtering. Let's take a look at how we can pipeline cmdlets together to list, filter, and sort the process list without the get-process cmdlet ever having to know what sorting is.

The Power of Composition

The phrase "the whole is greater than the sum of the parts" suits the idea of pipeline construction and composition very well. The pipeline makes it possible to take a number of small, effective components and combine them together to form a richer processing engine.

It's usually possible to break a task down into several distinct steps. Instead of trying to attack the whole lot at once, we can look at the first step and get it working fully. With that in place, we can focus all attention on the next step, and so on. Building up a pipeline in this fashion tends to be less fallible and, over time, becomes an efficient way to develop and reuse scripts for many different purposes.

How Do I Do That?

As we're already comfortable with the get-process cmdlet, we'll use that as a starting point. We'll create a pipeline with the | symbol and introduce the where-object cmdlet to apply a test to each object as it passes through the pipe. If the object satisfies the test criteria, it will continue on, in this case, to be shown in the console:

```
MSH D:\MshScripts> get-process | where-object { $_.Handles -gt 200 }

Handles  NPM(K)    PM(K)     WS(K) VS(M)   CPU(s)     Id ProcessName
-------  ------    -----     ----- -----   ------     -- -----------
    624      13    10548     15756    65    25.01   1656 CcmExec
    407       5     1684      3420    23    22.71    464 csrss
    274      11     7376     12696    55   565.91    212 explorer
    404      10     4472      2376    42    16.12    544 lsass
    282      12    35028     32416   176    21.93   3088 msh
    260       6     1276      2864    24    14.54    532 services
   1709      52    18092     24888   103    62.37    824 svchost
    209       6     2080      4320    36     4.80    940 svchost
    262      14     1500      3988    34    11.43    756 svchost
    284       0        0       216     2    77.96      4 System
    551      61     7332      4136    51    19.24    488 winlogon
    225       8     6364      7888    66     3.00   1708 wuauclt
```

Pipelines aren't limited to two stages. Now that we've established the set of processes that have more than 200 open handles, we can pipe that set into another cmdlet that will sort the output based on handle count:

```
MSH D:\MshScripts> get-process | where-object { $_.Handles -gt 200 } | sort-
object Handles
```

Handles	NPM(K)	PM(K)	WS(K)	VS(M)	CPU(s)	Id	ProcessName
209	6	2080	4320	36	4.80	940	svchost
260	6	1276	2864	24	14.54	532	services
262	14	1500	3988	34	11.64	756	svchost
274	11	7376	12696	55	580.04	212	explorer
284	0	0	216	2	78.89	4	System
405	10	4472	588	42	16.28	544	lsass
407	12	34632	33052	175	23.16	3088	msh
408	12	18432	19221	99	20.01	3089	msh
414	5	1684	3420	23	24.42	464	csrss
551	61	7332	4136	51	19.34	488	winlogon
618	13	10352	15740	64	25.38	1656	CcmExec
1748	53	18312	24964	105	63.40	824	svchost

Sometimes it's convenient to group objects by some property after they've been sorted. Like sort-object, the group-object cmdlet takes a parameter to organize its output. For example, let's view the same list, but this time, group together the processes by name:

```
MSH D:\MshScripts> get-process | where-object { $_.Handles -gt 200 } |
group-object ProcessName
```

Count	Name	Group
3	svchost	{svchost, svchost, svchost}
2	msh	{msh, msh}
1	CcmExec	{CcmExec}
1	csrss	{csrss}
1	explorer	{explorer}
1	lsass	{lsass}
1	services	{services}
1	System	{System}
1	winlogon	{winlogon}

What Just Happened?

The three new cmdlets we've covered here are all similar in their behavior. At a high level, they all examine the objects in the pipeline and put some or all of them back into the pipeline in a different order. The where-object cmdlet is used to control whether an object continues through the pipeline or is dropped. In contrast, the sort-object cmdlet will output every object it sees, but it may do so in a different order after it has had the opportunity to rearrange the objects. Meanwhile, the group-object cmdlet will allow all objects to pass through but will do so after placing the objects in a container related to the grouping property.

The $_ notation can be read as "this." When used in the script block for the where-object test, it refers to the current object in the pipeline. The dot notation, $_.Handles, is used to access the properties of the object for this test. We'll look at objects and their properties in more detail shortly.

MSH offers a set of operators for performing comparisons. Several of the common ones are listed in Table 1-1; Appendix A contains the complete list. Note that the < and > symbols are used for redirection in the shell and cannot be used to perform less-than or greater-than comparisons.

Table 1-1. Comparison operators

Operator	Description
-gt	Greater than
-lt	Less than
-eq	Equal to
-ne	Not equal to

The important point to note here is that the get-process has no notion of sorting or filtering. In addition to significantly reducing the complexity of that cmdlet, it also has the overall benefit in that sorting and filtering now use a common syntax anywhere within the shell. Whereas today you have to learn a different syntax for each tool (look at the differences in sorting between DIR and TLIST, for example), now it's just a case of using where-object and sort-object for everything.

What About...

...Using legacy tools in the pipeline? Is this possible? Yes! MSH allows the use of non-cmdlet applications to form part of a pipeline, even though it is not able to deduce any structure from their output. As such, output from a legacy tool will take the form of a list of strings representing each line of the output. For example, the command ping 127.0.0.1 | sort-object is valid, but it probably won't yield the results you're hoping for. MSH will simply perform an alphabetical sort of all the lines of output and kindly return that to the screen.

Given the previous output, it would be hard to claim that the grouped output is easier to read. Fortunately, as we'll discover, there are several other cmdlets that can be used to tidy this up for display on-screen, in print, or in other applications. As we're beginning to see, the key factor here is that the data is grouped as we want it and any downstream cmdlets will only have to be concerned with presentation.

…How about sorting on more than one field? Although we only used a single property in this case, sort-object will take a comma-separated list of fields for sorting. If the values of the first are the same for two objects, the values in the second will be compared instead.

Where Can I Learn More?

The built-in help guides for the cmdlets introduced here have more details on their syntax and usage:

```
get-help about_pipeline
get-help where-object
get-help sort-object
get-help group-object
```

All of these scenarios are made possible through the shift toward structured objects instead of text. We'll take a look at objects and the pipeline in more detail starting in Chapter 3. In the meantime, we'll look at some of the more immediate benefits of MSH.

Display Data

So far, we've been building commands with little attention to the output, other than assuming it will be displayed in the console window. How does MSH know how to neatly display the objects, especially if it's not familiar with their structure? It turns out that there is a fair bit of plumbing in MSH to make sure that console output is displayed in a useful form for a wide range of types.

The *default formatter* is a standard part of the shell. If and when an object reaches the end of the pipeline, MSH inspects its type and compares it to a list of known objects. If a match is found, MSH understands how to best format the object for display; if not, MSH displays the .NET properties of the object.

The type of the first object to reach the end of the pipeline generally governs how subsequent objects will be displayed. Alternatively, a command or script can explicitly insert formatting cmdlets (from the format-* family) and/or outputting cmdlets (from the out-* family) in the pipeline for more explicit control over how and where objects should be displayed.

Let's take a look at some of the different tools available for presenting data.

How Do I Do That?

Armed with the knowledge that there is a default formatter at work, we can look at the output of get-process in a new light. The default formatter knows about Process objects because they are one of the common data types used in shell work. The default formatter is configured to pick out some of the more interesting aspects of a process and tabulate them for display:

```
MSH D:\MshScripts> get-process

Handles  NPM(K)    PM(K)    WS(K) VS(M)    CPU(s)     Id ProcessName
-------  ------    -----    ----- -----    ------     -- -----------
    123       5     1008     2500    32      1.24   1844 alg
    799      14    14188    16480    71    189.09   1656 CcmExec
     19       1     1444     1516    13      1.61   1052 cmd
    426       5     1796     3148    24    184.88    464 csrss
    361      11     9420    13312    58  2,206.90    212 explorer
...
```

Some of the columns in this output, such as ProcessName and Id, are simple properties of the Process data structure. Others, including the non-paged memory size, paged memory size, and working set, are *calculated columns*. For each of these columns, the default formatter is running a small fragment of script on each Process object it sees, in this case, to convert a number in bytes to kilobytes for display.

We'll come back to the default formatter's behavior shortly. Meanwhile, let's say we're just interested in displaying a subset of the properties of the msh process. The format-list cmdlet is one of the simplest formatters. When provided with a list of property names, it will display each in sequence, along with its corresponding value. For now, let's just use a few properties that are common to all Process types; we'll see where these property names come from later when we meet the get-member cmdlet in Chapter 3:

```
MSH D:\MshScripts> get-process msh | format-list
ProcessName,PriorityClass,Id,VirtualMemorySize,Handles,StartTime,WorkingSet,
Modules

ProcessName        : msh
PriorityClass      : Normal
Id                 : 3088
VirtualMemorySize  : 186503168
Handles            : 451
StartTime          : 1/22/2005 5:20:51 PM
WorkingSet         : 37068800
Modules            : {msh.exe, ntdll.dll, mscoree.dll, KERNEL32.dll,
                      ADVAPI32.dll, RPCRT4.dll, SHLWAPI.dll, GDI32.dll,
                      USER32.dll, msvcrt.dll, mscorwks.dll, MSVCR80.dll,
                       mscorlib.ni.dll, ole32.dll, shell32.dll, comctl32.dll,
                      comctl32.dll, rsaenh.dll, mscorsec.dll, WINTRUST.dll,
                      CRYPT32.dll, MSASN1.dll, IMAGEHLP.dll, SOFTPUB.DLL,
                      xpsp2res.dll, userenv.dll, VERSION.dll, secur32.dll,
                      netapi32.dll, cryptnet.dll, WLDAP32.dll, WINHTTP.dll,
                      SensApi.dll, Cabinet.dll, System.Management.Automation.
...
```

format-table is one of the more versatile formatters. In simple usage it can be provided with a comma-separated list of properties and will automatically tabulate the corresponding values for each object it sees. In many cases, a simple format-table pass will be sufficient for data presentation:

```
MSH D:\MshScripts> get-process | format-table Id,ProcessName,StartTime

  Id ProcessName            StartTime
  -- -----------            ---------
1844 alg                    1/22/2005 5:17:58 PM
1656 CcmExec                1/22/2005 5:17:56 PM
1052 cmd                    1/29/2005 5:32:20 PM
 464 csrss                  1/22/2005 5:17:34 PM
 212 explorer               1/22/2005 5:19:06 PM
   0 Idle
 544 lsass                  1/22/2005 5:17:36 PM
3088 msh                    1/22/2005 5:20:51 PM
...
```

As with most formatting cmdlets, format-table will accept a GroupBy parameter. When displaying results, this is used to separate objects based on some property value. For cleanliness of presentation, it's common to first sort the input before presentation so that each grouped category appears just once. For example, let's create a tabulated process listing grouped by process priority:

```
MSH D:\MshScripts> get-process | sort-object PriorityClass,ProcessName |
format-table -GroupBy PriorityClass
ProcessName,Id,VirtualMemorySize,PriorityClass
```

```
   PriorityClass: Normal

ProcessName                              Id        VirtualMemorySize
-----------                              --        -----------------
svchost                                 896                 29769728
svchost                                 756                 35753984
svchost                                 824                110878720
svchost                                 720                 59514880
smss                                    308                  3911680
spoolsv                                1088                 27459584
svchost                                 940                 39124992
wmiprvse                                320                 23642112
wmiprvse                               1920                 26124288
wuauclt                                1708                 68648960
System                                    4                  1941504
csrss                                   464                 25485312
explorer                                212                 60772352
alg                                    1844                 33259520
CcmExec                                1656                 73891840
cmd                                    1052                 13979648
notepad                                1792                 25735168
services                                532                 25305088
msh                                    3088                186503168
lsass                                   544                 43470848


   PriorityClass: High

ProcessName                              Id        VirtualMemorySize
-----------                              --        -----------------
winlogon                                488                 53092352
Idle                                      0                        0
```

We've only scratched the surface of format-table here. It's possible to be far
more expressive in terms of formatting (width and alignment), as well as
content (through the use of calculated columns). In the following example,
the syntax may seem somewhat obtuse to begin with, but it's very regular
and can be used to create almost any imaginable table output:

```
MSH D:\MshScripts> get-process | format-table @{expression="ProcessName";
width=50; label="Name"}, @{expression="Id"; width=5}, @{expression={$_.
VirtualMemorySize/1024}; width=30; label="Virtual memory (kb)"}

Name                                         Id    Virtual memory (kb)
----                                         --    -------------------
alg                                        1844                  32480
```

CcmExec	1656	72008
cmd	1052	13652
csrss	464	24888
explorer	212	59348
Idle	0	0
lsass	544	42452
msh	3088	182132
notepad	1792	25132
...		

What Just Happened?

We started by looking at how the default formatter operates on known types. It's important to realize that the formatting process is applied to any object when it has nowhere further to go (i.e., it has reached the end of the pipeline, and the next stop is the console output). The shell does not discriminate between a single command (a pipeline of length 1, if you will) and a complex series of processes all piped together—ultimately, both cases have an end point.

format-list is a simple case, and we've already seen the bulk of its functionality here. One thing to remember is that because it generates the same listing for each element, its output can tend to get very large when it's used for any more than a small number of objects. It has a couple of other interesting usages. For types known to MSH, format-list with no parameter will display the object's most relevant properties, whereas format-list with a wildcard parameter (*) will display all of them. If the default formatter does not recognize a type it encounters, it always falls back to the list formatter that shows all properties and values of the object.

The complex format-table case uses a construct known as a *hashtable*, which is a data type we haven't discussed yet. When we look at hashtables and other data types in Chapter 3, we'll be able to revisit this aspect of format-table to create some more interesting reports.

What About…

…Are there any other formatters? The format-wide cmdlet can be used to list output in a horizontal order. Its formatting is similar to the effect of the /w switch on the DIR command where items are listed left to right and wrap when a line is complete.

…Combining grouping and the default formatter? It certainly is possible. If a formatting cmdlet is used without parameters and the objects are of a known type, the default formatting rules will be applied. In other words, applying format-table to the output of get-process will result in the familiar tabulated style offered by the default formatter. A pipeline such as get-process | sort-object PriorityClass | format-table –GroupBy PriorityClass can be used to group processes by priority while maintaining the standard column format.

Where Can I Learn More?

You can learn more about how the default formatter works by looking at the *.mshxml* file distributed with MSH. This file references a series of similar files, each of which contains configuration that is used by the default formatter.

The get-command cmdlet, as well as the help system, can also be used to find more information about the available formatters and their usage:

```
MSH D:\MshScripts> get-command format-*
```

What's Next?

By now, you've hopefully got a taste for the power of MSH as a tool. In the chapters that follow, we'll look more deeply into the different facets of the environment, starting with the basics and moving on to talk about the different components in more detail. Welcome aboard!

## CHAPTER 2

Customizing MSH

Now that we've seen a handful of the features that MSH has to offer, it's time to settle in and become familiar with the new environment. In this chapter, we'll look at some of the practical tasks that will save a lot of time in the future.

Load and Save Scripts

All of the examples so far have followed the same procedure: MSH presents a prompt and waits for your input, you type a command, the command is processed, the output is displayed, and the cycle repeats. This is useful for interactive command line use, invoking cmdlets one by one, building pipelines, and general day-to-day use.

However, like *cmd.exe*, MSH can take its instructions from a file instead of receiving commands from a keyboard. This enables us to create complex sequences that perform one or more tasks and save these scripts to disk. In this way, it's possible to build up a library of scripts that encapsulate common repetitive tasks. With this library on hand, it's easy to save time and quickly recall and rerun previously stored scripts.

Creating a Script Library

There are often cases where what appears to be a one-off script can actually be applied to many scenarios that crop up in the future. Saving scripts with well-chosen filenames that follow the verb-noun syntax of cmdlets can be a real timesaver. If possible, it's a good idea to keep scripts as generic as possible to increase the opportunities for reuse in the future.

How Do I Do That?

MSH scripts can be stored in simple text files with a *.msh* extension in much the same way as command-shell scripts can be stored in text files with a *.bat* or *.cmd* extension. Using your favorite text editor, let's put together a simple script that filters the output of get-process. Save the script, shown in Example 2-1, as *get-processHandlesGt500.msh* in a convenient directory. (We'll use *D:\MshScripts* in the examples that follow.)

Example 2-1. get-processHandlesGt500.msh

```
get-process | where-object { $_.Handles -gt 500 }
```

Once saved, the script can be run in the shell simply by typing in its path and name. If the script is located in the current working directory, the current path must also be specified as .*get-processHandlesGt500.msh*:

```
MSH C:\> D:\MshScripts\get-processHandlesGt500.msh

Handles  NPM(K)    PM(K)     WS(K) VS(M)   CPU(s)     Id ProcessName
-------  ------    -----     ----- -----   ------     -- -----------
    788      14    13832     16132    70   202.02   1656 CcmExec
    764      12    36760     34084   175    20.41   1864 msh
   1792      54    22476     24336   106   418.00    824 svchost
    557      60     7352      3820    51    58.92    488 winlogon
```

It doesn't stop there: with MSH, a script is part of a pipeline. For example, if we want to rearrange the results of the script and present them differently, it's simply a case of piping to the relevant cmdlets we've already met:

```
MSH C:\> D:\MshScripts\get-processHandlesGt500.msh | sort-object Handles |
format-list ProcessName,Handles

ProcessName : winlogon
HandleCount : 557

ProcessName : CcmExec
HandleCount : 785

ProcessName : msh
HandleCount : 800

ProcessName : svchost
HandleCount : 1792
```

Now, let's move to a slightly longer example. We'll create a new script, *get-processReport.msh*, as shown in Example 2-2, that generates a quick snapshot of the current process state and calls out high-priority processes in a separate list.

Example 2-2. get-processReport.msh

```
#
# This script generates a report about active processes
#

"Report generated at " + (get-date)
""                      # insert blank line

"Processes sorted by handle count"
get-process | sort-object Handles | format-table

""                      # insert blank line

"High memory usage (>100MB)"
get-process | where-object { $_.WorkingSet -gt 50000000 } | format-table
```

This time, let's run the script from the current working directory, after making sure that we're in the right folder (*D:\MshScripts*):

```
MSH D:\MshScripts> .\get-processReport.msh

Report generated at 12/1/2005 3:41:06 PM

Processes sorted by handle count

Handles  NPM(K)    PM(K)    WS(K) VS(M)   CPU(s)     Id ProcessName
-------  ------    -----    ----- -----   ------     -- -----------
   4344      75   138108   100852  1093 ...82.52   7404 OUTLOOK
   1785      54    21852    23708   106   414.66    824 svchost
    788      14    13980    16452    70   201.03   1656 CcmExec
    560      12    35252    32584   175    17.43   1864 msh
    557      60     7352     3820    51    57.46    488 winlogon
    438       5     1832     3212    24   236.38    464 csrss
    438      10     4728     2228    42    77.94    544 lsass
    363      11     9420    13324    58 2,582.09    212 explorer
    296       0        0      168     2   328.87      4 System
    266      13     1524     3264    34    94.29    756 svchost
    261       6     1316     2276    24    41.11    532 services
    248       7     2192     2996    37    19.84    940 svchost
    222       7     6356     6152    65    10.47   1708 wuauclt
    182       5     2316     3276    57     5.83    720 svchost
    137       3     1564     3420    23     3.98    320 wmiprvse
    132       3     3480     3204    25     9.67   1920 wmiprvse
    123       5     1008     2500    32     1.44   1844 alg
     96       4     2428     2364    26     2.19   1088 spoolsv
     89       4     1064     2252    29    10.04    896 svchost
     25       2      600     2228    25     1.10   3572 notepad
     25       2      692     2472    25     5.61   1792 notepad
     21       1      168      264     4     1.31    308 smss
      0       0        0       16     0                 0 Idle


High memory usage
```

```
Handles  NPM(K)    PM(K)      WS(K) VS(M)  CPU(s)     Id ProcessName
-------  ------    -----      ----- -----  ------     -- -----------
   4344      75   138108     100852  1093 ...82.52   7404  OUTLOOK
```

What Just Happened?

MSH recognizes script files by the *.msh* extension. Upon coming across a
script file, MSH will open the file and execute the commands within it line
by line. A script isn't any different from typing commands into the shell by
hand; it uses the same idea and execution order of a pipeline and is subject
to the same output-formatting rules, although there are some subtle differences caused by *scoping* (which we'll discuss in Chapter 4).

In Example 2-1, note that the objects representing the four processes from
get-processHandlesGt500.msh are actually emerging from the script into the
pipeline. In this manner, it's easy to blend script output with interactive
mode and build a pipeline that seamlessly includes aspects of both.

Assuming you may reuse a script in the future, it's always good practice to
add comments to areas where the behavior might not be immediately obvious later. If you come back to a script in six months, will you still remember
exactly why you chose to sort by a given property? Comments can be added
to a script by using the pound symbol, #. Once a # symbol appears on a line,
any characters following it (on the same line) are ignored when the script is
run. To the same end, it's a good practice to use the long form of commands (e.g., get-childitem instead of gci or dir) for legibility.

The get-date cmdlet hasn't been introduced yet, but its name should betray
its function. When used without parameters, it returns the current system
date and time in the short format (as defined by the system's Regional
Settings).

In the final version of MSH, a tighter security policy will be
enforced around script execution. Unlike the beta builds,
scripts will not be permitted to execute unless they are
signed with a trusted certificate.

MSH provides two cmdlets that assist with the signing process. get-authenticodesignature shows information about
the signature on a script, whereas set-authenticodesignature
is used to actually apply the signature.

The following steps are required to sign a script:

```
MSH D:\MshScripts> $cert = get-childitem cert:\
CurrentUser\My -CodeSigning
```

```
MSH D:\MshScripts> set-AuthenticateSignature
myscript.msh $cert
```

It is a good practice to get into the habit of signing scripts to
prevent accidental modification or malicious tampering.

What About...

...Running scripts as Scheduled Tasks? MSH has a command-line option, -command, that takes the filename of a script to run. Instead of loading up into interactive mode, it will immediately execute the script and exit:

```
msh -command D:\MshScripts\get-processHandlesGt500.msh
```

In fact, even the -command part is optional, so just passing the full filename is sufficient:

```
msh D:\MshScripts\get-processHandlesGt500.msh
```

What's more, if the *D:\MshScripts* folder is in the %PATH% environment variable, just the filename is enough:

```
msh get-processHandlesGt500.msh
```

In addition to the simple script invocation format with just a path and filename, there's another method called *dot sourcing*. A script file can be dot sourced by placing a period and space (.) before the script's filename. The distinction is important when variables and functions are used within the script, as the two methods treat variable and function scope differently. We'll look at dot sourcing more in Chapter 3.

After moving scripts into a file, it can be difficult to see what exactly is happening, especially when debugging. MSH has a debugging system that can help.

Try set-mshdebug -trace 1 to report each line of the script as it is run. Change the 1 to a 2 to have MSH report variable assignments as well. set-mshdebug -step can be used to walk through scripts line by line.

Where Can I Learn More?

Running the command msh -? will give more details about the available command-line options.

Save Keystrokes with Aliases

Isn't it odd that cd, dir, and echo still work in MSH? These commands don't follow the regular verb-noun format for cmdlets, yet MSH will happily work with them. This is an example of aliases at work. An *alias* is a mapping from one string to another, usually used to map a short name to any longer name for convenience.

When running the dir command, MSH is silently translating it to get-childitem (the equivalent cmdlet) and running that instead. This feature helps to shorten command length (and keystrokes) and bridge the syntax gap for the transition to MSH.

It's easy to set up your own aliases for commonly used commands.

A Word of Caution

Aliases can be a remarkably effective way of obscuring the behavior of a command or script, so it should be used sparingly. While it's certainly true that once you've defined a few aliases it's quier to type gps | so | ms | fl, do think of others (and yourself!) in the position of trying to understand exactly what's going on.

Although aliases are great for saving keystrokes, heavy use of very specific aliases within a script can render it less portable. If the functioning of a script depends on a whole list of custom alias mappings to be in place, it may be more difficult to transfer the script to other machines or share it with others without a long set-alias sequence at the start.

Using full cmdlet names (in long verb-noun format) is a good habit to get into and, as hard as it may be, leaving behind the legacy aliases such as dir, ls, and ps will help to make your scripts more universally readable.

How Do I Do That?

Let's start by taking a look at the default aliases. With no parameters, the get-alias cmdlet lists all active aliases:

```
MSH D:\MshScripts> get-alias
```

CommandType	Name	Definition
Alias	ac	add-content
Alias	clc	clear-content
Alias	cli	clear-item
Alias	clp	clear-property
Alias	clv	clear-variable
Alias	cpi	copy-item
Alias	cpp	copy-property
Alias	cvpa	convert-path
Alias	epal	export-alias
Alias	epcsv	export-csv
Alias	fc	format-custom

```
Alias       fl                          format-list
Alias       foreach                     foreach-object
Alias       ft                          format-table
Alias       fw                          format-wide
Alias       gal                         get-
...
```

That's quite a list. If we're just interested in finding out what the echo alias actually maps to, we can pass an alias to get-alias to single out only that mapping:

```
MSH D:\MshScripts> get-alias echo

CommandType   Name                      Definition
-----------   ----                      ----------
Alias         echo                      write-object
```

The set-alias cmdlet is used to create mappings, and it takes two parameters: first the alias and second the arbitrary target name. Maybe echo is still too many keystrokes and we'd prefer something more concise:

```
MSH D:\MshScripts> set-alias e write-object
MSH D:\MshScripts> e "Hello, World!"
"Hello, World!"
```

What Just Happened?

MSH stores its alias mappings in a simple lookup table that translates one string to another. When run, MSH first looks at a command for any aliases and then replaces them with their corresponding target. After that step is complete, MSH then looks for cmdlets, functions, and other shell constructs that are necessary to execute the command.

It's perfectly valid for aliases to take the same verb-noun form as cmdlets. Indeed, this can prove useful when overriding a cmdlet or rewiring the default verb. As we've seen, if a cmdlet is invoked without a verb, the get action is assumed. This behavior isn't always desired. For example, the location command could be used to set the location, instead of returning it, by defining set-alias location set-location.

Aliases can refer to other aliases or functions; after all, they're just a mapping from one string to another. It's also possible for an alias to refer to a non-existent target; in such cases, you won't find out about any alias-mapping problems until you try to use it.

 MSH doesn't check whether your alias is meaningful. A mistake in the set-alias statement might go undetected until you try to invoke it, so make sure an alias works as expected before depending on it.

As an alias can only point to one target at a time, the set-alias cmdlet will overwrite any previous alias mapping. It's possible to remove user-defined aliases from the mapping table with the remove-item alias:myalias command, although the built-in aliases such as gps (for get-process) cannot be changed. The built-in aliases are set up when the shell starts and will always be available. To get the list of constant aliases, use the following command:

```
MSH D:\MshScripts> get-alias | where-object { $_.Options -band [System.
Management.Automation.ScopedItemOptions]::Constant }
```

Because names for files, aliases, cmdlets, and other programs can potentially overlap, MSH follows a strict sequence of evaluation to determine what it's meant to do. The following order is used:

Alias
> Alias replacement occurs first, as previously described.

Function/filter
> We'll look at functions further in Chapter 3.

Cmdlet
> Cmdlets are the last internal command type in the shell to be checked.

Scripts
> If none of the previous three makes a match, MSH looks for scripts (with extension *.msh*) in the directories in the %PATH% environment variable.

Other programs
> If none of the previous four makes a match, MSH again looks through the directories in the %PATH% environment variable for any file with an extension defined in the %PATHEXT% environment variable. Generally, this includes *.com*, *.exe*, *.bat*, *.cmd*, and a few other file types like those used by *cmd.exe*.

 In a typical configuration, the current directory is not included in the path. Therefore, scripts and other programs might not be found, even if the current working directory contains a script or executable file with a matching name.

What About…

…Including parameters in the alias definition? There are plenty of cases where it would be convenient for an alias to refer to another command and pre-fill some of its parameters. For example, suppose I want to define an archive alias that used the copy-item cmdlet but always prepopulates the target folder. Aliases are simple in their design and cannot be used for this; they're a mechanism for bringing speed and/or consistency to command invocation. However, another MSH feature, functions, can be used to solve this need and many more. We'll look at functions in the next chapter.

…Can multiple aliases point at the same cmdlet? They can. If you'd rather use `displaytext` to insert objects into the pipeline, feel free to create an alias for it. Either `alias displaytext write-object` or `alias displaytext echo` would work well.

…Finding out which aliases refer to a given cmdlet? The `get-alias` cmdlet puts the shell alias table into the pipeline. We can use the trusty `where-object` to filter the mappings to just look for those that we're interested in. For example, we've seen a lot of `get-process` so far, so let's see whether the profile defines any aliases for it:

```
MSH D:\MshScripts> get-alias | where-object {$_.Definition -eq "get-process"}

Command Type    Name                    Definition
------------    ----                    ----------
Alias           gps                     get-process
Alias           ps                      get-process
```

Can aliases be used in a script? Aliases are available throughout the shell and work just as well in a script as elsewhere. However, it's important to realize that the use of aliases can potentially make scripts less portable. If a script relying on a certain alias is taken to a different machine or run by a different user, it's not guaranteed that the mapping will be in place, and the script may fail. As MSH moves away from legacy aliases, such as `dir` and `cd`, it's a good idea to get into the habit of using the long form of the cmdlet name in scripts.

Where Can I Learn More?

The `get-command` cmdlet can be used with a command-line option `-Noun` as in `get-command –noun alias` to return a list of alias-related cmdlets. As always, `get-help` provides more information about the complete usage of these cmdlets.

Work with the Command Line

Because *cmd.exe* runs in the Windows console subsystem, it inherits a number of features useful for command-line editing. The ability to edit the current command, as well as recall previous ones, proves to be a useful tool when working in an interactive command shell (and this feature continues to work in MSH). In this short section, we'll look at some of the standard editing keystrokes, as well as changes in the history buffer, that MSH offers.

The Legacy of DOSKEY.EXE

There was a time when DOSKEY was a vital part of any startup script on an interactive system. Building on the simple "recall last command" behavior, DOSKEY extended the command line with rich history, recall, and editing features. Instead of just recalling the last line, it suddenly became possible to recall any of the previous instructions. Fixing a typo in a previous command was also made easier, with the ability to move left and right along the input and inserting, deleting, or changing characters as needed.

In recent operating systems, the Windows console continues to support the same set of rich command editing and recall features with built-in functionality. MSH inherits this wholesale—the keystrokes and function keys retain their special powers throughout an MSH session.

Although DOSKEY remains a complement to *cmd.exe*, its other functionality deals with macros, a feature that is wholly overshadowed by the rich scripts and functions available in MSH.

How Do I Do That?

Command-line editing makes life a lot easier when entering commands in interactive mode. Suppose you've missed a parameter; no problem, just use the left arrow key to move back to the correct position and insert it. Need to fix a typo? Same idea. Use the cursor key to move to the correct position and then use Delete or Backspace to make any necessary changes. Other familiar shortcuts, such as Ctrl-left arrow, Ctrl-right arrow, Home, and End, will skip between words and go to the start and end of the command line, respectively.

When in interactive mode, every command entered is stored in what is known as the *history buffer*. The idea of a history buffer isn't new and is available in most command-line interpreters available today. As with most shells, the up and down arrows can be used to navigate through the history buffer, recalling previously executed commands and bringing them to the current command line. Also present is the Page Up/Page Down mapping to recall the first and last entries in the history buffer, respectively. Function keys also play their part, from F3 copying the remainder of the previous command into the current command line to F7 displaying a list of all history items in a pop-up box. Try them out, and you'll find that all of the command-prompt keystrokes continue to behave as expected.

MSH takes the history buffer one step further. The `get-history` cmdlet lists the content of the history buffer by placing `HistoryInfo` objects into the pipeline. From there it's only a short step to start using some of the familiar cmdlets for sorting and filtering, really making the history work for you.

As an example, let's take the case where we executed a command some time earlier and would now like to rerun it. Instead of browsing through the history by hand, let's set where-object to display the likely candidates:

```
MSH D:\MshScripts> get-history | where-object {$_.CommandLine -like "get-*"}

  Id CommandLine
  -- -----------
  75 get-process
  77 get-childitem -Recurse -Filter *.bak | sort-object Name
  82 get-location
 102 get-location
```

There it is: history item 77. Now we can use the invoke-history cmdlet to recall and execute the command line immediately:

```
MSH D:\MshScripts> invoke-history 77
get-childitem -Recurse -Filter *.bak | sort-object Name


    Directory: FileSystem::D:\MshScripts

...
```

There's one other useful trick to rely on when using interactive mode. So far, all of the interactive mode examples we've encountered have fit on a single line. However, when working with many instructions, it will often be more convenient to put different instructions on each line. To stop MSH from trying to run the first line as soon as Enter is pressed, we use the escape character (`` ` ``) at the end of the first line. This indicates that we're not quite ready yet and MSH should wait for all lines to be entered, followed by one last empty line, before running the command:

```
MSH D:\MshScripts> get-childitem `
| where { $_.Extension -eq ".txt" }
| sort Name
| format-table Name, Extension
# equivalent to
# get-childitem | where { $_.Extension -eq ".txt" } | sort Name | format-
table Name, Extension
```

In many cases, MSH is able to see that a continuation is needed—for example, if a line ends with a pipe symbol or inside a function definition. In these cases, MSH switches to the line continuation behavior until it sees an empty line.

We'll look at the other uses of the special `` ` `` character in Chapter 4.

What About...

...Increasing the size of the history buffer? By default, the history buffer stores only the last 64 commands, but this is easily changed. The limit is stored in an MSH variable called $MaximumHistoryCount. We'll look at variables more in the next chapter, but for now we can expand the buffer size by changing this value to a larger number:

```
MSH D:\MshScripts> $MaximumHistoryCount=1024
```

...Dumping the last few commands into a script file? If you've just entered a series of commands by hand but would like to keep the commands for reuse at a later date, it's easy to format the output of get-history for script generation. Let's say we'd like to store the last six commands into a script for future use. The Count parameter takes a number value corresponding to the number of entries to return, counting backward from the most recent:

```
MSH D:\MshScripts> get-history -Count 6 | format-table -HideTableHeader
CommandLine

cd \mshscripts\tutorials
delete *.bak
cd \mshscripts\samples
delete *.bak
cd \mshscripts\walkthroughs
delete *.bak
```

It's possible to redirect this output to a script by adding >D:\MshScripts\ remove-backups.msh (or something similar) to the end of a pipeline. If the commands you're trying to save are scattered through the history, it might be easier to call get-history without any parameters and cut and paste the relevant commands in a text editor.

There is one additional feature that MSH brings to the command-line editing experience: rich tab completion. From an empty command line, pressing the Tab key will insert the filename of the first file in the current directory onto the command line. Pressing it again will replace it with the next file, and so on, just like *cmd.exe*. However, MSH takes tab completion a step further and also offers completion of cmdlet names. Typing get-pro[Tab] will complete the get-process, while get-[Tab] can be used to cycle through all get-* cmdlets.

Where Can I Learn More?

The full list of DOSKEY keystrokes is supplied in the Windows XP documentation at *http://www.microsoft.com/resources/documentation/windows/xp/ all/proddocs/en-us/doskey.mspx*. Although the DOSKEY syntax isn't used in

MSH (it's replaced by aliases and functions), the keyboard shortcuts remain relevant.

More information on the get-history and invoke-history cmdlets is available through get-help.

By this point, we've seen a number of ways to customize the environment. Next, we'll take a look at the profile script and see how we can make these customizations available every time the shell is started.

Make Yourself at Home

For anyone who has spent significant time working in a shell, one thing quickly becomes apparent: there are some tasks that you repeat continuously until you finally break down and automate them with a script, often to be run at startup. Customizing your environment and creating your own shortcuts can significantly reduce the time spent on repetitive tasks and broaden the toolset at hand for solving new problems.

In this section, we'll look at a special script called the *profile* that can be used to customize the shell. We'll bring together some of the techniques we've already covered, in addition to a couple of new ones, and we'll create a script file that will be run every time the shell is started.

Moving in

As it installs, MSH targets the typical user, creating aliases and running other tasks that are applicable to just about anyone. However, everyone has his own habits when it comes to a command shell, and the out-of-box configuration is, by definition, very generic.

It's hard to say exactly what customizations to make given their personal nature. As a rule of thumb, if you find yourself repeatedly setting up the same aliases or functions, or performing the same tasks from session to session, those things are probably great candidates for inclusion.

How Do I Do That?

It's time for the text editor again. We'll create a file called *profile.msh* in the MSH directory of your *My Documents* folder. We can edit this file as we would any other script, but its name and location have special meaning: when MSH starts up, it will look for this script and run it. For now, let's write a script that configures some aliases, sets up a couple of useful functions, and prints a welcome message, as shown in Example 2-3.

Example 2-3. profile.msh in My Documents\MSH

```
# my personal aliases
set-alias ms get-member
set-alias prop get-property
set-alias displaytext write-object

# my personal functions
function prompt { "$((get-date).Month)/$((get-date).Day) " }
function day { (get-date).Day }

# increase the history buffer size
$MaximumHistoryCount=1024

# welcome message
"Welcome to MSH, " + $env:Username
```

That's it. Next time you start the shell, the customizations enacted by *profile.msh* will be present, and you'll be greeted with a friendly welcome:

```
Microsoft Command Shell
Copyright (C) 2005 Microsoft Corporation. All rights reserved.

Welcome to MSH, andy
8/15 $
```

 If you find that your profile grows in complexity over time, consider breaking it apart into separate files. Each might serve a different purpose: one might set up aliases; another might define a few common functions; and a third might define some functions and variables specific to a build system. The master profile can be used to weave all of the components together by dot sourcing each in turn.

. $MyDocuments\msh\aliases_profile.msh

. $MyDocuments\msh\functions_profile.msh

. $MyDocuments\msh\buildenv_profile.msh

What Just Happened?

After the shell has loaded, but before it can accept user input or run any scripts, it goes about setting up its execution environment. From a logical point of view, this is done in three distinct stages.

During the first stage, MSH runs the internal startup scripts and the system-level profile, which are stored in the *Documents and Settings\All Users\MSH* folder. This script takes the bare bones shell and makes it recognizable by defining a number of useful environment variables, familiar aliases, and commonly used functions.

The second case is the main extensibility point (the one that we explored here). Putting customizations into a separate file makes them more manageable, easier to port to newer versions of MSH, and more convenient for copying to other machines.

The third profile type enables a different profile script to be run when MSH is started on a specific machine or when it's based on some other criteria, such as access mode (imagine different behaviors based on whether you are accessing a machine physically or via a Terminal Services session). If you're set up with a roaming profile, it's sometimes convenient to create different profile scripts for the various machines you use, perhaps for the purpose of registering different file shares or modifying the available aliases.

In this section, we also touched on a new concept—functions. Because the next chapter covers functions, we won't dwell on them here, but the prompt function is worthy of mentioning. By default, the MSH prompt includes the current location when waiting for input, such as *cmd.exe*. Instead of using a separate program or special escape sequences to customize the prompt, MSH can evaluate a script each time user input is needed. To this end, MSH evaluates the prompt function, which contains a script. Because this function is run every time the prompt is shown, it's a good idea to keep the script fast and simple; otherwise, you'll be waiting for it to evaluate after every command.

Where Can I Learn More?

As you become more familiar with functions in the next chapter, you'll want to add the useful ones to your profile for easy access.

There's one additional topic we need to cover before exploring more of the new features in MSH.

Find Out What a Command Will Do Before Running It

MSH introduces several so-called *ubiquitous parameters* that are available throughout the command shell. Three important ones, -Verbose, -WhatIf, and -Confirm, tell you exactly what's going on, tell you what should be going on and check whether you'd like it to be going on (respectively) when running any MSH command. They can be used to get a better picture of how a script will perform before it is run, allowing you to verify the actions before they are performed.

Let's take a look at some of these safeguards in action.

I Wonder What This Button Does...

Picture this: You have an extensive folder structure containing a number of important files. Intermingled with these files are backups, or older versions, that really shouldn't be there. It makes sense to write a housekeeping script to walk through the structure and remove any files with a *.bak* extension. You've written the script and tested it on a simple (separate) test folder structure. Now you point it at the real folder and give it a whirl, only this time the results aren't quite as good as you expected. Alas, it's time to "try out" those disaster-recovery procedures. Something went wrong, but it's not entirely clear how or where. Surely there has to be a better way.

Thankfully, MSH has a few universal features that allow an administrator to ponder the "what if?" question, rather than the "what now?" question.

How Do I Do That?

Using the get-childitem cmdlet, it's an easy task to walk through a folder tree and pick out the files that match a certain criteria. Casting caution aside, you could pipe that output into remove-item to delete the matching files. This could remove more files than expected, however, so it's a good idea to use the -WhatIf switch to see what would happen before making any irreparable changes:

```
MSH D:\MshScripts> get-childitem . *.bak -Recurse | remove-item –WhatIf
What if: Operation "Remove File" on Target "test.bak"
What if: Operation "Remove File" on Target "reports.bak"
What if: Operation "Remove File" on Target "authors.bak"
What if: Operation "Remove File" on Target "contracts.bak"
What if: Operation "Remove File" on Target "accounts.bak"
```

The list looks good—none of these files should be there. Now it's time to rerun the command, this time without the -WhatIf switch, to remove the redundant files. Because this command is going to affect a large number of files, it makes sense to keep a log of the changes made in case any problems surface later. The -Verbose switch is used to instruct remove-item to explicitly report the files that it is deleting. If we so choose, it's easy to send this output into a file for record keeping:

```
MSH D:\MshScripts> get-childitem -Recurse -Filter *.bak | remove-item
-Verbose
Operation "Remove File" on Target "test.bak"
Operation "Remove File" on Target "reports.bak"
Operation "Remove File" on Target "authors.bak"
Operation "Remove File" on Target "contracts.bak"
Operation "Remove File" on Target "accounts.bak"
```

Because these parameters are ubiquitous, they work almost anywhere and with many different cmdlets. Suppose we have a number of open Internet Explorer windows and would like to close a couple of them. We can build a pipeline that will send all IEXPLORE instances to stop-process, but this time we'll use the -Confirm switch to ensure we only close those processes that we've finished using:

```
MSH D:\MshScripts> get-process iexplore | stop-process -Confirm
Confirm
Continue with this operation?
Operation "stop-process" on Target "iexplore (316)"
[Y] Yes  [A] Yes to All  [N] No  [L] No to All  [S] Suspend  [?] Help
(default is "Y"):y

Confirm
Continue with this operation?
Operation "stop-process" on Target "iexplore (2176)"
[Y] Yes  [A] Yes to All  [N] No  [L] No to All  [S] Suspend  [?] Help
(default is "Y"):y
```

What Just Happened?

The -WhatIf, -Verbose, and -Confirm options can change the behavior of the cmdlets to which they're applied. As a cmdlet receives an object from the pipeline, it may do either more or fewer actions, depending on the object type, the cmdlet, and the presence of these options.

 It's important to realize that while these options are suggested standards, they are not enforced or tested by MSH. Cmdlet and script authors are expected to respect these options if they are present, and most standard cmdlets treat them as described in this section.

However, when starting to use a new or unfamiliar cmdlet, it is a good idea to check that the cmdlet author's definition of -WhatIf aligns with your own.

-WhatIf can be used safely in almost all cases, as it explicitly tells the cmdlet to report what it would do without making any real changes. It's often convenient to redirect the output of a -WhatIf test to a file for review before committing any changes to disk, the registry, or other persistent store.

-Verbose provides detailed information about the operation of a cmdlet and is useful for storing a log of the script's activity. By itself, this log cannot be used to undo changes, but it may be invaluable at a later date as an aid to data recovery or process auditing.

-Confirm allows a manual go/no-go decision for each step in the process. Of course, if a script is going to be processing tens of thousand of items, it may be more economical to inspect the output of -WhatIf and make any changes to the script or underlying store if the behavior isn't perfect. With that said, -Confirm can be useful in cases where a smaller set of items is being processed or in instances where accidental execution of a command can have severe consequences.

What About...

...Using multiple ubiquitous parameters on the same command? Although it is permissible to include both -WhatIf and -Confirm switches on the same command, it's not recommended. The switches are all interrelated in their purpose, so their combination results in one switch overriding another. For example, when both -WhatIf and -Verbose are used, -Verbose is effectively ignored because the -WhatIf switch generates equivalent output. Likewise, when -WhatIf and -Confirm are combined, the explicit yes/no questions of -Confirm will still be raised and an affirmative response will commit a change.

Can you apply this behavior across all cmdlets? Yes. The $WhatIfPreference and $ConfirmPreference variables can be used to change the default settings of the -WhatIf and -Confirm options for those cmdlets that support them.

...Are there any other ubiquitous parameters? MSH cmdlets often support a number of other parameters that all serve different purposes. The -? option is available universally and is equivalent to invoking get-help on the cmdlet name.

What's Next?

Now that you're settled in and comfortable in these new surroundings, it's time to take a look at some more MSH features, including variables, functions, and language constructs such as conditional tests and loops.

CHAPTER 3

Scripting MSH

In this chapter, we'll discuss some of the core MSH language features that complement the features we've already covered, as well as how they can be used to build more powerful scripts. As we'll be looking at the basic building blocks, some of the examples may appear rather abstract. However, we'll keep the examples short and simple to help introduce the behavior and purpose of these new features. We'll waste no time putting these new constructs to work as we move forward.

Before we begin, let's look at how the .NET Framework fits into the picture.

The .NET Framework

Although the .NET Framework is invariably described in terms of C# and VB.NET—two programming languages that rely on the infrastructure they provide—it's not just for developers. There are a number of facets to the framework, including a *Common Language Runtime* (CLR), which provides a common set of functionality to all .NET applications and tools. Compilers for the .NET programming languages generate *managed code*, which is a set of instructions understood by the CLR. When it comes time to run the managed code, the CLR converts it into native executable instructions (suitable for the architecture of the machine) and actually runs it. This whole process is largely transparent to both the developer and the end user. To complement the runtime, there is a broad *Class Library* that contains all kinds of useful functions and data types.

Although MSH itself is written as managed code, the only important takeaway is that the .NET Framework redistributable is needed for any MSH work. However, for our purposes, there are two key aspects of the .NET Framework that we'll see in MSH time and again: strongly typed structured objects and the Class Library.

Most command-line administrative shells, such as *cmd.exe*, have just one or two data types: strings and integers. Creative use of strings and integers has resulted in some really clever scripts, but interoperation and portability between different processes is often bound by a strict contract such as the exact format of string. The .NET Framework defines not only a number of standard data types, including strings and integers, but also Booleans (true/false), floating point numbers, and arrays (an ordered collection of many items of the same type). We call variables that are declared with these types *strongly typed*, meaning that if a variable claims to be a double precision floating-point number, we can be confident that it really is a number and not a string or something else. There's no need to check that the data inside a floating-point number is actually in the correct format because the .NET Framework handles that.

In addition to these strongly typed variables, the .NET Framework introduces the idea of a *class*, which is a container that encapsulates a number of data types to represent something altogether more complex. Take a date and a time that could be represented by the string 03/29/2001 18:44:01. This is fine in the simple case, but it falls apart when we want to compare one hour with another; then, we need to resort to string parsing. Now instead, imagine a DateTime class that has separate *properties*—integers, in this case—for each of the elements of the string: year, month, day, hour, minute, and second. The class defines the structure of data; when it's populated with some real values, we call it an *object*.

For example, the output of get-date is a DateTime object. Checking (get-date).Hour is a lot more convenient than converting the 12th and 13th characters of a string to a number. Classes can also have *methods*, which perform some action on the data contained inside. Two examples from the DateTime class include AddDays, which shifts a date by a number of days (correctly observing month and year boundaries), and ToUniversalTime, which returns the same instant in UTC.

The Class Library provides a wide set of auxiliary functionality, much of which is just as useful to a script author as it is to a developer. Instead of having to use addition, subtraction, and many tests, the DateTime class lets us compare the difference between two dates with ease. Similar classes exist for text manipulation, URL parsing, low-level network communication, XML work, and many other common tasks. Given its broad scope, the Class Library is divided into *namespaces*—logical groups of classes—that are summarized on MSDN at *http://msdn.microsoft.com/library/default.asp?url=/library/en-us/cpref/html/cpref_start.asp*. Many of the built-in cmdlets are built on top of this infrastructure, exposing its usefulness but hiding the underlying plumbing from view.

Now, let's get back to MSH and see how all of this comes together.

Work with Structured Objects

Just as a DateTime object has properties for year, month, day, and so on, so too do the other types we've already seen. The Process class includes process ID, name, and other information, and the get-process cmdlet generates a sequence of objects, one for each process running on a system, with each of these values set accordingly. It's not immediately obvious from the output of get-process how much information is lurking within these objects. Next, we'll see that there's far more than just process name and ID.

Let's take a more detailed look at what these objects contain and how—with just the few cmdlets we've discussed so far—there's much more information waiting to be tapped.

Just How Much Information Is in There?

Judging by the output of the cmdlets we've discussed so far, there are plenty of useful properties to work with—but that's just the beginning. For common data types (including processes, files, and directories), the default formatter has a list of some typical properties. It's these properties that are shown in most of the output so far, but as we'll see in this section, the classes we've been using contain a wealth of information that isn't shown immediately. Fortunately, there are cmdlets that let us access just about any piece of the information we need.

How Do I Do That?

With all of the information stored inside these objects, we need a guide—something that will help us get more familiar with these new data structures we're working with. The get-member cmdlet is here to make life easier. With no parameters, it lists every detail about the object. For the following examples, we'll be focusing on the properties (the "public" values and settings). Therefore, we'll tell get-member to just return those:

```
MSH D:\MshScripts> get-process | get-member -MemberType Property

    TypeName: System.Diagnostics.Process

Name                       MemberType Definition
----                       ---------- ----------
BasePriority               Property   System.Int32 BasePriority {get;}
```

```
ExitCode                   Property   System.Int32 ExitCode {get;}
HasExited                  Property   System.Boolean HasExited {get;}
ExitTime                   Property   System.DateTime ExitTime {get;}
Handle                     Property   System.IntPtr Handle {get;}
HandleCount                Property   System.Int32 HandleCount {get;}
Id                         Property   System.Int32 Id {get;}
MachineName                Property   System.String MachineName {get;}
MainWindowHandle           Property   System.IntPtr MainWindowHandle {get;}
MainWindowTitle            Property   System.String MainWindowTitle {get;}
MainModule               Property    System.Diagnostics.ProcessModule MainM...
MaxWorkingSet              Property   System.IntPtr MaxWorkingSet {get;set;}
MinWorkingSet              Property   System.IntPtr MinWorkingSet {get;set;}
Modules                  Property    System.Diagnostics.ProcessModuleCollec...
NonpagedSystemMemorySize   Property System.Int32 NonpagedSystemMemorySize ...
NonpagedSystemMemorySize64 Property System.Int64 NonpagedSystemMemorySize6...
PagedMemorySize            Property   System.Int32 PagedMemorySize {get;}
PagedMemorySize64          Property   System.Int64 PagedMemorySize64 {get;}
PagedSystemMemorySize     Property    System.Int32 PagedSystemMemorySize {get;}
PagedSystemMemorySize64   Property    System.Int64 PagedSystemMemorySize64 {...
PeakPagedMemorySize        Property   System.Int32 PeakPagedMemorySize {get;}
PeakPagedMemorySize64     Property    System.Int64 PeakPagedMemorySize64 {get;}
PeakWorkingSet            Property    System.Int32 PeakWorkingSet {get;}
PeakWorkingSet64          Property    System.Int64 PeakWorkingSet64 {get;}
PeakVirtualMemorySize     Property    System.Int32 PeakVirtualMemorySize {get;}
PeakVirtualMemorySize64   Property    System.Int64 PeakVirtualMemorySize64 {...
PriorityBoostEnabled      Property    System.Boolean PriorityBoostEnabled {g...
PriorityClass            Property     System.Diagnostics.ProcessPriorityClas...
PrivateMemorySize         Property    System.Int32 PrivateMemorySize {get;}
PrivateMemorySize64       Property    System.Int64 PrivateMemorySize64 {get;}
PrivilegedProcessorTime   Property    System.TimeSpan PrivilegedProcessorTim...
ProcessName               Property    System.String ProcessName {get;}
ProcessorAffinity    Property    System.IntPtr ProcessorAffinity {get;s...
Responding                Property    System.Boolean Responding {get;}
SessionId                 Property    System.Int32 SessionId {get;}
StartInfo              Property    System.Diagnostics.ProcessStartInfo St...
StartTime                 Property    System.DateTime StartTime {get;}
SynchronizingObject   Property    System.ComponentModel.ISynchronizeInvo...
Threads                 Property    System.Diagnostics.ProcessThreadCollec...
TotalProcessorTime      Property    System.TimeSpan TotalProcessorTime {get;}
UserProcessorTime       Property    System.TimeSpan UserProcessorTime {get;}
VirtualMemorySize         Property    System.Int32 VirtualMemorySize {get;}
VirtualMemorySize64       Property    System.Int64 VirtualMemorySize64 {get;}
EnableRaisingEvents       Property    System.Boolean EnableRaisingEvents {ge...
StandardInput             Property   System.IO.StreamWriter StandardInput {...
StandardOutput            Property   System.IO.StreamReader StandardOutput ...
StandardError             Property   System.IO.StreamReader StandardError {...
WorkingSet                Property    System.Int32 WorkingSet {get;}
WorkingSet64              Property    System.Int64 WorkingSet64 {get;}
Site                     Property    System.ComponentModel.ISite Site {get;...
Container                Property    System.ComponentModel.IContainer Conta...
```

Back to the output of get-process we saw earlier, it's clear that there is more information than the default view shows. For example, process names such as svchost and lsass can often be too cryptic to immediately understand their purpose. We can use a new cmdlet, select-object, to pick out a couple of interesting properties—in this case, the process name and its longer description:

```
MSH D:\MshScripts> get-process | select-object ProcessName,Description

ProcessName                      Description
-----------                      -----------
alg                              Application Layer Gateway Service
CcmExec                          CCM Executive
cmd                              Windows Command Processor
cmd                              Windows Command Processor
csrss
explorer                         Windows Explorer
Idle
lsass                            LSA Shell (Export Version)
msh                              msh
notepad                          Notepad
notepad                          Notepad
ntvdm                            NTVDM.EXE
regedit                          Registry Editor
services                         Services and Controller app
smss                             Windows NT Session Manager
...
```

As we've already seen, get-process can take a parameter for matching a process name; in this case, we'll specify msh. By enclosing the cmdlet and parameters in parentheses, we're now able to access properties on the object that it returns:

```
MSH D:\MshScripts> (get-process msh).Threads


BasePriority           : 8
CurrentPriority        : 8
Id                     : 1716
IdealProcessor         :
PriorityBoostEnabled   : True
PriorityLevel          : Normal
PrivilegedProcessorTime : 00:00:01.0414976
StartAddress           : 2011608519
StartTime              : 5/20/2005 4:26:17 PM
ThreadState            : Ready
TotalProcessorTime     : 00:00:04.7167824
UserProcessorTime      : 00:00:03.6752848
WaitReason             :
ProcessorAffinity      :
Site                   :
Container              :
```

```
BasePriority              : 8
CurrentPriority           : 8
Id                        : 1136
IdealProcessor            :
PriorityBoostEnabled      : True
PriorityLevel             : Normal
PrivilegedProcessorTime   : 00:00:00
StartAddress              : 2011608507
StartTime                 : 5/20/2005 4:26:17 PM
ThreadState               : Wait
TotalProcessorTime        : 00:00:00
UserProcessorTime         : 00:00:00
WaitReason                : UserRequest
ProcessorAffinity         :
Site                      :
Container                 :

BasePriority              : 10
CurrentPriority           : 12
Id                        : 916
IdealProcessor            :
PriorityBoostEnabled      : True
PriorityLevel             : Highest
PrivilegedProcessorTime   : 00:00:00.8412096
StartAddress              : 2011608507
StartTime                 : 5/20/2005 4:26:17 PM
ThreadState               : Wait
TotalProcessorTime        : 00:00:03.9657024
UserProcessorTime         : 00:00:03.1244928
WaitReason                : UserRequest
ProcessorAffinity         :
Site                      :
Container                 :
...
```

Now let's take a look at another set of data associated with each process: its
Modules property, which is a collection of all of the assemblies and DLLs
used by the process. Because that's probably going to be a long list, we'll use
where-object to select just those that are greater than 5 MB in size:

```
MSH D:\MshScripts> (get-process msh).Modules | where-object
{$_.ModuleMemorySize -gt 5M}

    Size ModuleName                                          FileName
    ---- ----------                                          --------
  5,076k mscorwks.dll                                        C:\WINDOWS\Mic...
 10,392k mscorlib.ni.dll                                     C:\WINDOWS\ass...
  8,256k shell32.dll                                         C:\WINDOWS\sys...
  7,696k System.ni.dll                                       C:\WINDOWS\ass...
 10,512k System.Xml.ni.dll                                   C:\WINDOWS\ass...
  6,776k System.Data.ni.dll                                  C:\WINDOWS\ass...
```

What Just Happened?

get-member is useful for finding out property names and values if you're not familiar with the class you're dealing with. Because Process objects have many properties and methods, we used the MemberType parameter to select just a subset. Feel free to explore the output when no member type is specified. You'll see how much information is available from a seemingly simple command.

From what we saw in the previous section, it seems as though get-member should be run on every running process (since there will be a corresponding object for each in the pipeline). If that's the case, why did we see the properties only once? As get-member is commonly used on a stream of identical classes, its default behavior is to list only the members of a type it hasn't seen yet. If, for some reason, you need get-member to list for every type, this behavior can be overridden with the -ForEachObject option.

select-object is a useful tool for simplifying objects as they pass through the pipeline. Given a number of properties of interest, it will take these from each object it sees and create a simple new object with just these fields. This can bring about performance gains (since the new objects are significantly smaller) and simplify downstream processing.

Here we also see a new concept—the idea of a *collection*. When dealing with the Threads property, instead of seeing just a single value (as we did with ProcessName, for example), we get back a sequence of objects, one for each of the threads in the process. These objects are put into the pipeline, in order, which means that we can now use the familiar, group-object, sort-object, and where-object cmdlets on this data.

What About...

...Supplying other properties to select-object? In the previous example, ProcessName and Description might not be the two most useful fields to select. By all means, feel free to pick out other properties to meet your own needs; any of the properties revealed by get-member are fair game:

```
MSH D:\MshScripts> get-process | select-object Id,Name,Threads
```

...Using MSH to determine which processes are using a certain module? By combining a handful of cmdlets together, we can filter the Modules list to select just those processes that match specific criteria. Let's say we're interested in finding all processes using the Crypto API that is located in the file *crypt32.dll*. We use the -Expand option on select-object to break each process's Modules collection into separate ProcessModule objects. Instead of the whole Modules collection going into the pipeline in one big chunk, each of the ProcessModule objects will go through in turn (accompanied by the Id and ProcessName properties of the parent Process):

```
MSH D:\MshScripts> get-process | select-object Id,ProcessName –Expand
Modules | where-object {$_.ModuleName -eq "CRYPT32.dll"} | select-object
Id,ProcessName
```

Collections have properties that differ from those of the objects they contain. Looking back at the contents of the Threads property output, it's clear that there are a number of threads; we saw the details of each in turn. The option -InputObject on get-member can be used to inspect the Threads collection rather than the properties of the ProcessThread objects it contains:

```
MSH D:\MshScripts> get-member –InputObject (get-process msh).Threads


     TypeName: System.Diagnostics.ProcessThreadCollection

Name             MemberType Definition
----             ---------- ----------
Count            Property   System.Int32 Count {get;}
get_Item         Method     ProcessThread get_Item(Int32 index)
Add              Method     Int32 Add(ProcessThread thread)
Insert           Method     Void Insert(Int32 index, ProcessThread thread)
IndexOf          Method     Int32 IndexOf(ProcessThread thread)
Contains         Method     Boolean Contains(ProcessThread thread)
Remove           Method     Void Remove(ProcessThread thread)
CopyTo           Method     Void CopyTo(ProcessThread[] array, Int32 index)
get_Count        Method     Int32 get_Count()
GetEnumerator    Method     IEnumerator GetEnumerator()
GetType          Method     Type GetType()
ToString         Method     String ToString()
Equals           Method     Boolean Equals(Object obj)
GetHashCode      Method     Int32 GetHashCode()
```

Note that we couldn't just do (get-process msh).Threads | get-member; that would have caused *automatic expansion* of the Threads collection, resulting in get-member showing the properties of the individual objects contained within. As it stands, we see that the Threads collection has a Count property that seems to be what we're looking for. Using the same dot notation as earlier, we can easily get a tally of the threads in use. Note that you might get a different number of threads when trying this on your own machine—that just shows that the expression is returning the number of threads running inside your MSH process:

```
MSH D:\MshScripts> (get-process msh).Threads.Count
7
```

Where Can I Learn More?

The built-in help for the two new commands we've covered in this section has further usage information:

```
MSH D:\MshScripts> get-help get-member
MSH D:\MshScripts> get-help select-object
```

Store Information in Variables

So far we've been building increasingly complex command-line sequences to solve problems. Even with only the aspects of MSH that we've discussed thus far, it's clear that we've already got quite a toolkit. However, in some cases, it becomes important to maintain some state while processing is underway. Think about making modifications to a subset of thousands of files and needing to keep a record of those that have changed. What if you had a lookup mechanism that could associate a person's full name, email address, and other details with his or her username? This is a scenario in which you might want to take the output of one pipeline and run it into two or more separate ones.

Whether data is needed for decision making during execution or will be used as part of a result or audit after completion, we need somewhere to keep this data for later use. Variables are the mechanism by which MSH allows us to maintain state during processing. Variables are a place to store objects; along with the data they hold, they maintain a sense of the objects' type and structure. Variables can be used to store just about anything, from numbers to filenames to sequences, all the way up to collections of objects.

We'll begin here with a few simple scenarios to become familiar with variable usage and syntax. By the end of the chapter, we'll bring everything together and see how variables, combined with conditional tests and functions, add an extra layer of versatility for solving problems.

Variables Have Types, Too

Variables provide a place to store objects and can be used to store almost any piece of data used in the command shell. Instead of relying solely on the pipeline for moving data around, we can store objects for later use.

Although it isn't necessary to say exactly what information a variable will store beforehand, as soon as a variable is assigned a value, it takes on a type. Variables are objects, too, and they can be used in the pipeline and acted upon by cmdlets such as get-member. They also support the dot notation for accessing their properties.

How Do I Do That?

Variables in MSH are identified with the $ prefix. This helps separate variables from cmdlets, aliases, filenames, and other identifiers used in the shell. There is no forced naming convention for variables, although it's always good practice to use a name that actually represents the information stored within; if nothing else, it can dramatically help readability and understanding of scripts later on. Variable names are always case-insensitive, and they can contain any combination of alphanumeric characters (A–Z and 0–9), as well as the underscore (_) character.

Let's start with some simple arithmetic and a variable called number:

```
MSH D:\MshScripts> $number = 1      # create a variable and give it a value
MSH D:\MshScripts> $number
1
MSH D:\MshScripts> $number = 4*6    # replace the value
MSH D:\MshScripts> $number
24
MSH D:\MshScripts> $number += 2     # update the variable by adding two
MSH D:\MshScripts> $number
26
MSH D:\MshScripts> $number++        # increment the variable
MSH D:\MshScripts> $number
27
```

Text strings are treated in a similar fashion. Many of the same operators (such as addition and multiplication) translate directly:

```
MSH D:\MshScripts> $myString = "Hello"
MSH D:\MshScripts> $myString += ", World!"
MSH D:\MshScripts> $myString
Hello, World!
MSH D:\MshScripts> $myString = "Hello" * 6
MSH D:\MshScripts> $myString
HelloHelloHelloHelloHelloHello
```

With the basics in place, we can look at some of the richer data structures that variables enable. Arrays give us the power to store many pieces of information within a single variable. Simple arrays contain a sequence of data, often, but not necessarily, of the same type. We'll look at a sequence of numbers here, but it's important to remember that an array could just as easily be used to store a list of filenames for further processing or a sequence of ProcessInfo objects:

```
MSH D:\MshScripts> $arr = @(1,2,3,4)
MSH D:\MshScripts> $arr           # list the contents, one element per line
1
2
3
4
```

```
MSH D:\MshScripts> $arr.Count
4
MSH D:\MshScripts> $arr[2]          # get the third element ([0] is the first)
3
MSH D:\MshScripts> $arr = @(1,2)
MSH D:\MshScripts> $arr += 3
MSH D:\MshScripts> $arr
1
2
3
MSH D:\MshScripts> $arr = @(("a", "b"), 2, 3)
MSH D:\MshScripts> $arr[0]
a
b
```

Another useful data structure we'll begin to rely on is the *hashtable*, a special type of array where one value (the *key*) is associated directly with another (the *value*). Think of a hashtable like a dictionary: the key is the word you're looking up and the value is the definition that lives beside it.

Hashtables can be very useful for storing related data because, when provided with a key, they allow very fast lookup of a piece of associated information. In the following case, we build a hashtable of the relationship between machine names and their owners. When provided with a key, the associated value is easily retrieved from a hashtable:

```
MSH D:\MshScripts> $h = @{}               # create a new, empty hashtable
MSH D:\MshScripts> $h["hermes"] = "Andy"
MSH D:\MshScripts> $h["zeus"] = "Andy"
MSH D:\MshScripts> $h["hades"] = "John"
MSH D:\MshScripts> $h["poseidon"] = "Bob"
MSH D:\MshScripts> $h

Key                         Value
---                         -----
hermes                      Andy
zeus                        Andy
hades                       John
poseidon                    Bob

MSH D:\MshScripts> $h["zeus"]
Andy
```

Variables can be used to store just about any data structure used in the shell, including items that are passed through the pipeline. We can fill a variable using the same assignment operator (=) or by using the set-variable cmdlet at the end of a pipeline. It's often convenient to store information in a variable and then use it as the source for building a pipeline.

```
MSH D:\MshScripts> $allProcesses = get-process
MSH D:\MshScripts> $allProcesses | format-table Name
```

```
Name
----
alg
CcmExec
csrss
explorer
Idle
lsass
msh
...

MSH D:\MshScripts> get-process | where-object { $_.HandleCount -gt 200 } |
set-variable -Name MyProcesses
MSH D:\MshScripts> $MyProcesses.Count
12
MSH D:\MshScripts> $MyProcesses[0]
Handles  NPM(K)    PM(K)    WS(K) VS(M)   CPU(s)    Id ProcessName
-------  ------    -----    ----- -----   ------    -- -----------
    840      14    14572    15444    77   547.39  1656 CcmExec
```

One final important thing to realize is that for *value types*—such as integers,
strings, and arrays—assignment is done *by value*. Let's look at how this
works—we'll see the reasoning behind it in just a moment (as before, the 93
number returned from get-alias may be different depending on whether
you have set up any additional aliases):

```
MSH D:\MshScripts> $a = 10
MSH D:\MshScripts> $b = $a
MSH D:\MshScripts> $b
10
MSH D:\MshScripts> $a = 0
MSH D:\MshScripts> $b
10
MSH D:\MshScripts> $aliasesVar = get-alias     # $aliasesVar is an array
MSH D:\MshScripts> $aliasesVar.Count
93
MSH D:\MshScripts> new-alias wo where-object   # now 94 registered aliases
MSH D:\MshScripts> $aliasesVar.Count
93
```

In contrast, when a *reference type* like a hashtable, Process object, or
FileInfo object is assigned to a variable, assignment happens *by reference*.
Again, let's first see how this works and understand the behavior in a
moment:

```
MSH D:\MshScripts> $ht=@{a=10;b=20}
MSH D:\MshScripts> $ht

Key                     Value
---                     -----
a                       10
b                       20
```

```
MSH D:\MshScripts> $otherht = $ht
MSH D:\MshScripts> $otherht["c"] = 30
MSH D:\MshScripts> $ht

Key                     Value
---                     -----
a                       10
b                       20
c                       30
```

What Just Happened?

There are many ways to define and update variables. Basic assignments using the assignment operator (=) simply take the value from the righthand side and associate it with the variable name on the left. There are a series of other operators known as compound assignment operators that can be used to update existing variables based on their current value. Of these, we saw +=, which takes the current value of the variable, adds the righthand side to it, and updates the variable with its new value. Likewise, *= has a similar result but performs multiplication instead of addition. Table 3-1 lists the common compound assignment operators.

Table 3-1. Compound assignment operators

Assignment operator	Equivalent to	Effect
$x += $y	$x = $x + $y	Add and assign
$x -= $y	$x = $x - $y	Subtract and assign
$x *= $y	$x = $x * $y	Multiply and assign
$x /= $y	$x = $x / $y	Divide and assign

The other common mechanisms for updating numeric variables are the increment and decrement operators ($x++ and $x--, respectively). Equivalent to doing $x+=1 or $x-=1, these operators are a convenient shorthand.

Global variables, such as the ones we've seen here, are available from the moment they are defined until the shell is closed and are not persisted between different MSH sessions. There are other types of variables (such as local and script-scoped) that we'll explore at the start of Chapter 4.

Working with arrays and hashtables

An array is *index-based*, which means that each element is stored in sequence and can be accessed at a numeric location. The first item in the array has an index of zero, the second an index of one, and so on. An individual element is retrieved using square brackets containing the index number and appearing immediately after the array (e.g., $arr[13]).

Arrays can either be populated with values when first defined—with the @(element1, element2, element3) syntax—or updated after creation. Extending an array to contain a new element is as simple as using the += compound operator. Multiple elements may be added at once by adding two arrays together, forming a single array that comprises the elements of both. The range operator .. can also be used to fill an array with a range of values:

```
$a = @(1,2,3)
$b = @(4,5,6)
$c = $a+$b          # equivalent to $c=@(1,2,3,4,5,6)
$d = @(1..6)        # equivalent to $d=@(1,2,3,4,5,6)
```

Hashtables have obvious similarities to arrays with one significant difference: instead of using a numeric index, they use an arbitrary key. For this reason, it's not possible to iterate through the contents of a hashtable using a numeric index. Thus, hashtables expose two collections—Keys and Values—that contain the information stored within.

Like arrays, hashtables can be built up progressively as we saw previously, populated with data at creation time, or they can have multiple key-value pairs added at once through "hashtable addition":

```
$ht = @{hermes="Andy"; zeus="Andy"; hades="John"; poseidon="Bob"}
$ht += @{athena="Bob"; apollo="John"}
```

Special values

The special value $null is used to represent a null or undefined value. The null value is very flexible. If you add a number to it, it behaves as if it were zero. If you try to append a string to it, it will behave as if it were an empty string. Add a hashtable or array to null, and it behaves as if it were an empty hashtable or array. Setting a variable to null clears any previous value it might have held.

An empty array (one that contains zero elements) is represented by the @( ) syntax. Similarly, the @{} syntax (note the curly braces) is used to create an empty hashtable.

These special values are summarized in Appendix A.

By-value assignment

In effect, when an assignment is made with a *value type*, the variable is given a copy of its assignment at that instant. For simple variable types, such as numbers, this behavior is generally intuitive. However, in cases where cmdlets are used to populate an array of results, it's vital to remember that the cmdlet was run once, at assignment time, and any further use of the variable content is based on that copy. If you need the absolute latest output of a cmdlet, it is best to run it again rather than rely on a potentially old and out-of-date copy stored in a variable.

By-reference assignment

In the last example, we saw that even though the third element was added to the $otherht hashtable, it looked as though it was added to both $ht and $otherht. This difference from by-value assignment is easier to understand if you realize that there is just a single hashtable and both $ht and $otherht are references (or pointers) to it. Creating a third variable ($thirdht=$otherht) simply creates another reference; now there are three variables pointed at the same object.

What About...

...What happens if you use the same variable name in two places? Will they interfere with each other? It depends. We'll come back to some more advanced aspects of variables in the next chapter to see how MSH controls the access and visibility of variables through a system called scoping.

...Using $_ as a valid variable name? $_ is a valid variable name, although, as we saw earlier, the $_ variable has special meaning inside certain script blocks. With some cmdlets, such as foreach-object and where-object, a script block is used to operate on or make decisions about pipeline objects. In these cases, the $_ variable is pre-populated and contains the current pipeline object when the script block is run. Although it's valid to use $_ for other purposes, it's a better idea to use a more descriptive variable name outside of these cases.

...Using a variable before it has been assigned a value? Technically, it can be done, although it's rarely a good idea. If you use a variable that hasn't yet been assigned a value, you'll get a null value back and won't see any errors. This may seem to work out fine in some cases, but always consider whether your script will behave in the same way if the variable does have a value. In practice, it's always a good idea to set any variables to a known value (such as zero or an empty string) before using them.

...Seeing which variables you've defined? Yes. In the same way that we can browse through the registry like a filesystem, MSH creates a special drive that represents the assigned variables. You can use the standard commands to list the names and current values of any defined variables:

```
MSH D:\MshScripts> set-location Variable:
MSH D:\MshScripts> get-childitem
```

…Removing elements from a hashtable? The hashtable is a rich class that exposes several methods for manipulating the content stored within (all of which can be discovered with $ht | get-member –MemberType Method). The Remove method takes a key and removes it from the set, whereas the Clear method can be used to empty the hashtable entirely:

```
MSH D:\MshScripts> $ht = @{a=10;b=20;c=30}
MSH D:\MshScripts> $ht.Remove("a")
MSH D:\MshScripts> $ht

Key                         Value
---                         -----
b                           20
c                           30

MSH D:\MshScripts> $ht.Clear( )
```

Where Can I Learn More?

The language reference guides built into get-help offer a full list of arithmetic and assignment operators, as well as some more details on the various data structures available:

```
get-help about_Arithmetic_Operators
get-help about_Assignment_Operators
get-help about_Array
```

Control Script Flow with Comparisons

Now that we have all this state to work with, it's time to start making some decisions. We have already touched on how to make tests and comparisons in Chapter 1, and we'll be using the same operators here. In this section, we'll explore the if and switch statements and see how they can be used, depending on certain conditions, to execute different parts of a script.

Echoes of GOTO

Although flow control is possible in *cmd.exe*, its reliance on labels, simple IF tests, and GOTO commands can make for some complicated batch files.

With the if and switch constructs in MSH, controlling script flow becomes more intuitive and a lot easier to read after the fact. MSH doesn't carry over the concept of GOTO from *cmd.exe* because it simply isn't needed. Cases where GOTO is used in a batch file to send execution off to a section of reusable commands that can be replaced with functions is a concept we'll look at later in this chapter.

How Do I Do That?

Starting with some simple cases, let's make comparisons between two constants. This will lay the foundation for what is to come:

```
MSH D:\MshScripts> 7 -gt 5
True

MSH D:\MshScripts> 7 -eq 5
False

MSH D:\MshScripts> "alpha" -lt "zulu"
True
```

No surprises here. MSH is performing the comparison and putting a Boolean (true/false) value into the pipeline based on the outcome. Tests become more interesting when we compare a dynamic value against a constant one, but, in every case, a test will always generate a true/false value.

In this case, we'll compare the number of files in a given folder against an arbitrary value considered to be "many," and assign the result to a variable:

```
MSH D:\MshScripts> set-location c:\windows\system32
MSH C:\WINDOWS\system32> $lotsOfFiles = ((get-childitem).Count -gt 50)
MSH C:\WINDOWS\system32> $lotsOfFiles
True
```

The comparison operators provide the framework for determining things about the environment in which the script is running. Naturally, now that we're able to make decisions about state, we can put them into action and control the flow of execution. Our ally here is the if statement and its relations else and elseif:

```
MSH C:\WINDOWS\system32> if ((get-childitem).Count -gt 50) { "More than 50
items in this folder" }
More than 50 files in this folder
```

Let's build this up into a more complete example. The script in Example 3-1 checks the number of files in a folder against a known expected value and then reports its findings. In this example, we'll only run this check on the first day of the month (which would be useful if this formed part of a larger script that was run daily).

Example 3-1. DayOneReportCheck.msh

```
$statusReportCount = (get-childitem "D:\StatusReports").Count
$departmentCount = 23
$dayOfMonth = (get-date).Day

if ($dayOfMonth -eq 1)
{
    if ($statusReportCount -eq $departmentCount)
```

Example 3-1. DayOneReportCheck.msh (continued)

```
    {
        "All departments accounted for"
    }
    elseif ($statusReportCount -lt $departmentCount)
    {
        "Missing"+($departmentCount-$statusReportCount)+"reports"
    }
    else
    {
        "Too many reports found!"
    }
}
```

In Example 3-1, we've implicitly combined two tests: making sure it's the first day of the month and checking the number of reports. It's often convenient to collapse several tests into a single condition using the -and and -or operators. Example 3-2 has a different script that might be used as a reminder at the start of each month.

Example 3-2. DayOneCleanupReminder.msh

```
$dayOfMonth = (get-date).Day
$workingFiles = (get-childitem "$MyDocuments\Ongoing").Count

if (($dayOfMonth -eq 1) -and ($workingFiles -gt 50))
{
    "A new month is here; please clean out $MyDocuments\Ongoing."
}
```

The if statement on its own gives complete power to control what happens next, but there are situations in which there are several different ways to proceed, depending on a variable's value. Implementation of these more complex decisions with if statements can quickly lead to a tangled collection of elseif statements, which can be hard to read and maintain in the long run. In these cases, it can be more convenient to use a similar but different construct: the switch statement. The switch statement combines several tests into single blocks, and it generally makes such scripts easier to read, as shown in Example 3-3.

Example 3-3. DayOneReportCheckSwitch.msh

```
$statusReportCount = (get-childitem "D:\StatusReports").Count
$departmentCount = 23
$dayOfMonth = (get-date).Day

if ($dayOfMonth -eq 1)
{
    switch ($statusReportCount)
```

Example 3-3. DayOneReportCheckSwitch.msh (continued)

```
    {
        {$_ -lt 5}
        { "Very few reports present (<5)" }

        {$_ -gt 4 -and $_ -lt 10 }
        { "Many reports missing (5-10)" }

        {$_ -gt 9 -and $_ -lt 20 }
        { "Usual report count (10-20)" }

        {$_ -gt 19 -and $_ -lt 23 }
        { "Most reports present (>20)" }

        23
        { "Perfect" }

        default
        { "Unexpected number of reports present" }
    }
}
```

What Just Happened?

The comparison operators -gt and -lt appear consistently throughout the examples in this section and they, along with the other comparison operators, are the vital ingredient when controlling script flow. All comparisons result in a Boolean result where the outcome will either be true or false.

Comparison operators will work consistently on a wide range of data types. In all cases, the equality test -eq will be available, whether comparing numbers, strings, collections, or objects. For simple variable types such as numbers and strings, additional operators such as -gt and -lt become available (performing numeric and alphabetic comparisons, respectively). Other operators, such as -and and -or, are used for comparing Boolean types. We saw a few of the comparison operators in Chapter 1; the full list can be found in Appendix A.

Once we were able to define a conditional test to determine something about the environment, we looked at two language constructs used to control script flow. Let's take a look at these in more detail.

The if statement

The if statement takes the form of a condition followed by a script block. Not all parts of the following syntax are required and some may appear more than once:

```
if (<condition 1>)
{ <block 1> }
elseif (<condition 2>)
{ <block 2> }
else
{ <block 3> }
```

If <condition 1> is satisfied, the content inside of <block 1> will be run. Conditions are tested as Boolean values, and all comparison operators return results of that type. If <condition 1> wasn't met (it evaluated to false), flow skips over <block 1> and on to any elseif statements that might be present. Although elseif statements are not required, there may be any number of them present. Each elseif condition is evaluated in turn, and as soon as a match is found, the corresponding script block is run. If not one of the conditions is met, flow proceeds to the optional else block; the final <block 3> is run if it is present.

If any of the conditions are true, the corresponding block is executed. When that block is complete, the whole statement is finished and no further tests are performed. Even if several elseif conditions are true, only the block for the first will ever be run.

The switch statement

The switch statement, although similar to if, has a different syntax and a wider range of uses:

```
switch (<test variable>)
{
    <literal> { <block 1> }
    { <test block> } { <block 2> }
    default { <block 3> }
}
```

Every switch statement focuses on the idea of comparing the <test variable> against something else. The test could be a shell variable, a property, an object, or even a set of objects coming out of a pipeline.

Within the body of the switch statement, there are three types of comparisons that can occur:

Literal comparison
    If a literal (such as a number or string) is present, MSH effectively checks <test variable> -eq <literal> and will run <block 1> if the test evaluates to true.

Test block
> An expression is included in braces for evaluation. Inside the expression, $_ is used to represent the current *<test variable>* value. If the expression evaluates to true, the corresponding *<block 2>* is run.

Default
> The default keyword may only appear once in a switch statement and is equivalent to the else part of the if statement. *<block 3>* is executed if and only if none of the other matches are made.

Flow through a switch statement is notably different than the flow through an if statement. With a switch statement, where multiple matches are made, each of the corresponding script blocks is run in sequence. As a rule of thumb, if you can do it with an if and an elseif, you should. But if you find yourself needing many elseif cases or repetition in the script blocks, it's probably a good opportunity to rework the logic with a switch statement.

What About...

...Comparing incompatible types? What happens if you try to see whether a number is "greater" than a word? When MSH sees incompatible types in a comparison, it attempts to convert the second to the same type as the first, and then it compares the results. Order is sometimes significant here, so be careful, as the outcome may not always be what you expect:

```
MSH D:\MshScripts> (10 -gt "Hello")
The '-gt' operator failed: Cannot convert "hello" to "System.Int32". Error:
"Input string was not in a correct format."..
At line:1 char:8
+ (10 -gt  <<<< "hello")

MSH D:\MshScripts> ("Hello" -gt 10)
True
```

In the first case, MSH tries to convert the word "Hello" to a number and fails, stating the cause. However, note that in the second case, the number 10 is converted to a string without complaint. (This automatic conversion of numbers to strings is usually very convenient.) When strings are compared, the results depend on the alphabetical ordering of the characters within them. Because the digits are considered to occur before the alphabet, the digit 1 is seen as less than A, and therefore less than H; MSH does the best it can and returns a result based on this ordering.

Where Can I Learn More?

Get-help offers the full list of comparison operators with the keyword about_Comparison_Operators.

Do Repetitive Work with Loops

If there's one thing computers are good at, it's executing the same code over and over again. Looping is a powerful concept that can simplify many repetitive tasks. Using a loop, we can write a single block of script that is executed a multiple number of times based on some defined conditions. This lets us focus on getting the real logic working correctly in a single place and then easily scaling it out or applying it as needed. No longer are we constrained to the copying and pasting command sequences to perform the same actions on different files, folders, machines, or settings. Better still, any changes to the logic made once centrally will then be applied in each iteration the next time the script is run.

In the following examples, we'll look at populating a file structure with some report templates. We'll start by creating a report placeholder for each week and then move on to separating them out month by month.

Make MSH Work for You

Looping is a great way to save time: write the logic once and run it over and over again. The pipeline has allowed us to perform the same tasks repeatedly on different objects. When piping the output of get-process to where-object, MSH is running the where-object test on each object that flows through the pipeline.

The explicit looping language constructs we'll see here—for, foreach, and while—allow us to use the same kind of functionality on variables without invoking the pipeline directly.

How Do I Do That?

We'll use a couple of files in the following examples as sample report templates. From the interactive mode, enter the following commands to set up the environment for this example:

```
MSH D:\MshScripts> new-item -Name "Reports" -Type Directory
MSH D:\MshScripts> "Weekly report template" >WeeklyTemplate.txt
MSH D:\MshScripts> "Monthly report template" >MonthlyTemplate.txt
```

Now, with an empty *Reports* directory into which we'll soon place some reports and a couple of simple templates, we're ready to go. Fire up your favorite text editor and create a file called *new-weeklyReports.msh* with the script in Example 3-4.

Example 3-4. new-weeklyReports.msh

```
for ($week=1; $week -le 52; $week++)
{
    copy-item "WeeklyTemplate.txt" "Reports\Week $week.txt"
}
```

Run the script by typing the following command:

```
MSH D:\MshScripts> ./new-weeklyReports.msh
```

You can confirm that the script ran properly by opening the *Reports* folder in Explorer. Inside you should find 52 neatly arranged reports just waiting to be written.

Next, we'll take a look at the while construct. The script in Example 3-5 creates 12 directories and puts a copy of the template in each.

Example 3-5. copy-reportsToMonths.msh

```
$month=1
while ($month -le 12)
{
    $monthfolder = "2005-" + $month.ToString("00")

    # create the month folder
    new-item -Path "Reports" -Name $monthfolder -Type Directory

    # copy the template into it
    copy-item "MonthlyTemplate.txt" "Reports\$monthfolder\Summary.txt"

    $month += 1
}
```

After running the script, you should see this output:

```
    Directory: FileSystem::D:\Reports

Mode     LastWriteTime        Length Name
----     -------------        ------ ----
d----    Aug 19 00:55                2005-01
d----    Aug 19 00:55                2005-02
...
d----    Aug 19 00:55                2005-11
d----    Aug 19 00:55                2005-12
```

The command shell is giving feedback indicating that it has created each of the folders in the list. In reality, each time the new-item cmdlet runs successfully, it is putting a DirectoryInfo object into the pipeline, which MSH then displays in tabular form. Sure enough, the *Reports* folder in Explorer now shows an additional 12 subfolders, each containing a *Summary.txt* file.

Now, suppose you want to extend this system to include monthly reports filed by individual departments. This new requirement is easy to accommodate by making just a few modifications to the script. You start by creating an array to list the different departments and using the foreach statement to loop over each in turn, repeatedly executing a command block. The whole script is included in Example 3-6.

Example 3-6. copy-reportsToMonthsAndDepts.msh

```
$departments = ("Sales", "Marketing", "Research", "Support")

$month=1
while ($month -le 12)
{
    $monthfolder = "2005-" + $month.ToString("00")

    new-item -Path "Reports" -Name $monthfolder -Type Directory
    copy-item "MonthlyTemplate.txt" "Reports\$monthfolder\Summary.txt"

    foreach ($department in $departments)
    {
        copy-item MonthlyTemplate.txt "Reports\$monthfolder\$department.txt"
    }

    $month += 1
}
```

Running the script shows the same output in the command-shell window as the script in Example 3-5, indicating that each of the folders has been created. However, looking into the folders this time, the script modification has created an extra four reports in each month's folder.

What Just Happened?

We've looked at three different ways to have the command shell repeatedly execute a script block.

The for loop

Think of the for statement as having four parts:

```
for (<initialization>; <condition>; <repeat command>)
{ <block> }
```

The first three are included in the parentheses after the for statement and are separated by semicolons (although a newline can be used to separate them, too). The fourth, the script block, is enclosed in brackets and can contain any number of MSH commands.

The first part, the initialization statement, allows us to set up any variables we'll use in the loop. In this example, we defined a variable $week that started at 1.

The second part, the condition, is checked each time before the code block is run. If it evaluates to false, the loop is finished and execution moves to the line after the script block. If the condition isn't true when the loop is entered, the block will never run. In this case, you want the script to run until it reaches a week that is not less than or equal to 52.

The third component, the repeat command, is executed each time the end of the block is reached. This can be used to update any variables so that the loop runs differently the next time around. In our example, we need to walk through each week of the year, so we incremented the value of $week by one with each iteration.

The content of the block will be executed each time the loop is run.

The while loop

The while statement has just two parts, the condition and the block:

```
while (<condition>)
{ <block> }
```

Each time the loop is entered, the condition is evaluated. If it returns true, the block is run. The block will be run over and over until the condition no longer holds.

With both for and while loops it's important to make sure your condition will at some point not be true—otherwise, your script will be stuck in an endless loop, repeating the block until it is interrupted. This can be particularly bad if, for example, you're writing a new file to disk, printing a document, or sending an email inside the block. Always make sure that your loop will end when its work is done.

The foreach loop

The foreach statement iterates the elements of an array. Although this task could also be achieved with a for or while loop, the foreach statement is usually significantly easier to read and often much more efficient:

```
foreach (<element> in <elements>)
{ <block> }
```

On the first iteration, the variable named in <element> will be populated with the first item in the array. When the block finishes its first run, the variable <element> will be updated to contain the second element, and so on.

It was convenient in this example to define an array to contain the different departments as it could easily be extended in one place if the need were to arise in the future.

Formatting strings

For the curious, the `$month.ToString("00")` command returns a string that is formatted with a leading zero. This uses a feature of the string class in the .NET Framework. We'll look at some more uses of the Class Library in Chapter 5.

What About...

...Using the `if` statement within a loop? Absolutely. There are plenty of cases where a loop seems like a great solution but leaves you saying, "Do this each time except when...." Enter the `break` and `continue` commands. The sole purpose of these two commands is to disrupt the flow of execution. The `break` command immediately skips to the end of the innermost loop and doesn't come back. The script will start running immediately after the closing brace of the `for/while/foreach` block. The `continue` command also skips to the end of the innermost loop, but the loop may run again if the condition still holds true (or if there are additional elements in the array for a `foreach` loop). For example, the following script will skip every number divisible by 10:

```
foreach ($i in (1..100))
{
    if (($i % 10) -eq 0) { continue; }
    "$i is not divisible by ten"
}
```

Given three different constructs for building a loop, it's sometimes hard to pick the right one. The good news is that you're free to choose whichever construct best fits your needs. The previous `while` example could also be written to use a `for` loop (`for ($month=1; $month -le 12; $month++)`) or a foreach statement (`foreach (1..12)`).

The foreach-object cmdlet, which translates the foreach functionality into the pipeline, can be used to run a script block against every object in the pipeline—for example: `get-process | foreach-object { $_.HandleCount > "$($_.ProcessName).txt" }`. The foreach-object cmdlet is aliased as foreach for convenient use in the pipeline.

Where Can I Learn More?

As always, there are built-in help pages for each of the three looping constructs (about_for, about_while, and about_foreach). The execution flow commands are also there (about_break, about_continue). Looping with for and while relies heavily on conditional tests we explored earlier.

The string-formatting trick that used ToString is just one of the many things possible with the .NET Framework String class. More details about custom formatting of numeric strings are on MSDN: *http://msdn.microsoft.com/library/ default.asp?url=/library/en-us/cpguide/html/cpconcustomnumericformatstrings.asp.*

Capture Reusable Behavior in a Function

As we saw earlier, it's easy to start with several simple tasks and join them together to create increasingly complex scripts and pipelines. At some point, instead of using the recall buffer, it is convenient to store command sequences in scripts for later reuse. Functions serve a similar purpose by enabling us to collect one or more commands and group them together so that they may be run with a single command. What sets functions apart is that they can be used to return a result based on the processing of a set of inputs—in effect, the function becomes a black box that encapsulates some frequently used logic.

Several of the built-in commands, such as clear-host, are, in fact, functions that perform tests, determine parameters, and invoke cmdlets based on their inputs. The new-item cmdlet is very flexible, yet at the same time, it can have a cumbersome syntax; thus, MSH creates these short-cut functions for convenience. Even familiar commands such as C: and D: are functions that call the set-location cmdlet.

We'll see how functions offer the means to bring together the various topics we've seen in this chapter, including variables, conditional tests, and loops. Functions can range from the very simple to the surprisingly complex, yet they invariably offer a way to arrange scripts neatly in logical sections, making them much easier to understand and maintain than other methods.

How Do I Do That?

For our first function, let's start with something simple that prints out a welcome message:

```
MSH D:\MshScripts> function say-greeting { "Hello" }
MSH D:\MshScripts> say-greeting
Hello
```

The Black Box

Among their virtues, functions have one very strong value proposition: they neatly group together a piece of logic into a single place. Tasks well-suited to shell scripts frequently incur some repetition of logic, whether that involves extracting information from an object, storing data into a variable, or performing some calculations. Although the task may be simple, putting it into a pipeline or script with several other tasks can quickly cause that simplicity to vanish. Functions provide some refreshment by allowing a little bit of script to be taken aside and given a name. The opportunity to get that part working in isolation can make writing the overall script faster and debugging scripts a far more manageable task.

Functions are only as useful as the information they have at their disposal. Now, let's see how we can pass arguments to a function that it can then use for decision making. We'll extend the say-greeting function to optionally take a person's name. The param keyword is used to call out the parameters that are expected to be passed to the function on the command line:

```
MSH D:\MshScripts> function say-greeting {
>>param($name)
>>$message = "Hello, "
>>if (! $name) { $message += "World" }
>>else { $message += $name }
>>$message
>>}
>>
MSH D:\MshScripts> say-greeting
Hello, World

MSH D:\MshScripts> say-greeting Andy
Hello, Andy
```

Functions coexist neatly with cmdlets and aliases. Earlier we saw how aliases provide an alternative name for commonly used cmdlets. Functions can take this a step further, either by encapsulating a small pipeline or by prepopulating certain arguments for a cmdlet:

```
MSH D:\MshScripts> function get-ProcessByHandles {
>>param($count = 200)
>>get-process | where-object { $_.Handles -gt $count }
>>}
>>
MSH D:\MshScripts> get-ProcessByHandles 400 | format-list

ProcessName : CcmExec
Id          : 1656
```

```
ProcessName : csrss
Id          : 464

ProcessName : explorer
Id          : 492
...
```

Suppose we want to place a function into a pipeline. Inside the function script block, functions have a special variable $input. When a function is placed in a pipeline, the $input variable will be populated with any incoming objects before the function is run. To continue the pipeline inside a function, we can pipe $input into another cmdlet:

```
MSH D:\MshScripts> function get-properties {
>>$input | get-member -MemberType Property
>>}
>>
MSH D:\MshScripts> get-process | get-properties


    TypeName: System.Diagnostics.Process

Name                    MemberType Definition
----                    ---------- ----------
BasePriority            Property   Int32 BasePriority {get;}
ExitCode                Property   Int32 ExitCode {get;}
HasExited               Property   Boolean HasExited {get;}
ExitTime                Property   DateTime ExitTime {get;}
...
```

Functions become very powerful when used for processing and returning a result to the caller. For a function to return data, there is no need to explicitly call out "I want to return this value;" instead, the script block inside the function has the freedom to place any number of objects into the pipeline for downstream processes to use. In the next example, we'll see that by simply running a command that has output ($total), the function will generate a meaningful result.

Let's consider a simple function that adds together all command-line arguments. This time, we'll use the special variable $args, which is an array of all arguments passed to the function on the command line:

```
MSH D:\MshScripts> function add {
>>$total = $null
>>foreach ($arg in $args) { $total += $arg }
>>$total
>>}
>>
MSH D:\MshScripts> add
0
MSH D:\MshScripts> add 1 2 3
6
```

```
MSH D:\MshScripts> $b = (add 11 12 13)
MSH D:\MshScripts> $b
36
MSH D:\MshScripts> add "foo" "bar"
foobar
```

As we've seen, functions can invoke cmdlets, maintain their own state, and return results. Putting all of these aspects together, let's create a useful function for reporting disk usage within a folder (and, optionally, its subfolders). The get-childitem cmdlet does the bulk of the work for us; we just walk through its results and add the sizes of any files found. When we're done, we'll put the total count into the pipeline and let MSH take care of the rest:

```
MSH D:\MshScripts> function du {
>>$bytes=0
>>get-childitem -Recurse:($args[0] -eq "-r") | foreach { $bytes += $_.Length }
>>$bytes
>>}
>>
```

Normally, we'll want to see the results in kilobytes rather than bytes, but there's no need to duplicate the same logic in another function. Instead, just wrap du into another function that will do this conversion automatically:

```
MSH D:\MshScripts> function duk {
>>(du $args)/1k
>>}
>>
MSH D:\MshScripts> du
9959698

MSH D:\MshScripts> duk
9726.267578125
```

What Just Happened?

Functions are one of the most useful elements of the command shell in that they provide an easy framework for reusing scripts and logic across a wide range of tasks. Unlike cmdlets, no strict naming convention is enforced, although it's always good practice to use self-descriptive names. Whenever possible, try to name functions in the same verb-noun format, especially if they serve purposes similar to already existing cmdlets.

Functions separate from aliases at the point at which they can take input, either from the command line or when introduced into a pipeline sequence. In most cases, rather than using the $args variable directly, the param keyword should be used to identify explicitly the parameters that a function expects to receive. Using named parameters makes functions much more readable and easier to follow.

In one of the previous examples, the get-ProcessByHandles function gave one of its named parameters, $count, a default value: if no arguments had been passed to the function, $count would automatically have assumed a value of 200.

In Example 3-7, the add-integers function shows how the data types of parameters can also be identified in the param section. MSH takes care of ensuring that all parameters are of the correct type (integer) before running the main body of the function.

Example 3-7. add-integers function

```
function add-integers {
    param([int]$a, [int]$b)
    $a+$b
}
```

When a function is used in a pipeline, any cmdlets or processes will first complete all of their tasks before the function is run. The function will wait, collecting all of the input coming through the pipeline, and will not start until everything else before it has finished. Functions are executed in this way to ensure that the special variable $input will always contain the complete set of pipeline objects available to the function. In just a moment, we'll look at a special type of function called a *filter* that is sometimes more suited to pipeline use.

Not all functions are required to generate output. For those that do, the types of objects emitted by the function will depend on the purpose it serves. In our add example earlier, one result, a number, was returned at the end of the function. In other cases, for example, when a loop is involved, it may be more desirable to output data for each iteration of the loop. When multiple results are generated by a function, they'll be available in the pipeline for downstream processing in exactly the same order in which they were generated.

What About…

…Seeing the functions you've defined? As we saw with variables, the built-in *variable provider* exposes a Function: drive that contains all of the defined functions for the current session.

You set a variable in your function, but when you run the function, the variable is never set. What's going on? This is actually expected behavior and is another instance in which variable scoping comes into play. By default, variables set or defined within a function are only available within that function; when the function finishes, any variables settings are removed. This helps prevent a function from accidentally interfering with another function. We'll look at scoping more in Chapter 4.

Although all of the examples here used interactive mode, it's perfectly valid to use functions inside script files. It might be a good idea to add the definitions of frequently used functions to your profile so they'll be available whenever you need them.

Transform Objects as They Pass Through the Pipeline

Functions remain one of the most versatile aspects of the MSH language. Their use in both command-line and pipeline situations makes them very flexible. However, there are times when we're creating solely for pipeline use, and it's more convenient to run a script block on each object in the pipeline than getting them delivered in one large chunk in the $input variable. Let's say we're going through each line of a 400 MB daily IIS logfile to figure out the set of requested URLs that resulted in a 404 error message. Loading all 400 MB into memory probably isn't the best approach; we would do better to create a small script block that could match a 404 line in the log and record the requested URL into a variable.

To accommodate these cases, MSH offers a special type of function, called a *filter*, that is designed to be placed into the pipeline and used to inspect, modify, or augment data as it passes between processes.

Let's create a couple of filters to see how they work.

Functions and Filters

Given that functions and filters are defined with very similar syntax, have similar purposes, and can both operate in the pipeline, you'd be forgiven for asking, "Can't I just use a function for this?" The answer is yes: any purpose a filter serves can also be met with a function. Filters are convenient for situations in which the processing of individual pipeline objects is the key focus, and the filter can operate in isolation, without knowledge of what has come before or what will follow. Filters remove the need to loop over every item in the $input variable. Also, because a filter is run for each pipeline object rather than for the whole collection, filters can also show some significant performance gains over functions when processing large quantities of data.

How Do I Do That?

We'll start by defining a very simple filter. Filters are defined in the same way as functions, but instead of using arguments or $input, we again make use of the special variable $_:

```
MSH D:\MshScripts> filter double { $_ * 2 }
```

Let's take the new filter for a test drive. To begin, we'll use some simple values to seed the pipeline:

```
MSH D:\MshScripts> 10 | double
20

MSH D:\MshScripts> @(1,2,3,4) | double
2
4
6
8

MSH D:\MshScripts> @(1,2,3,4) | double | double
4
8
12
16
```

Let's stay with the number theme for one more example. In this case, we'll write a filter that expects a number and uses a loop to determine whether it's prime (i.e., whether any numbers other than itself will divide into it):

```
MSH D:\MshScripts> filter test-prime {
>>$limit = ($_/2)+1;
>>for ($i=2; $i -lt $limit; $i++)
>>{
>>   # divisible by $i, so drop this object and return
>>   if (($_ % $i) -eq 0) { return }
>>}
>>$_    # nothing divided into it, must be prime
>>}
>>
MSH D:\MshScripts> @(1..100) | test-prime
1
2
3
5
7
...
```

Fascinating, but how exactly are filters useful? For the next example, we'll use an MSH feature called notes. *Notes* can be used to attach a piece of data to an object as it passes through the pipeline. This note can then be accessed seamlessly by downstream cmdlets as if it were a property of the object.

Here, we'll create a filter that can recognize a few file extensions and attach a note to any `FileInfo` objects that pass through:

```
MSH D:\MshScripts> filter add-friendlytype {
>>switch ($_.Extension)
>>{
>>    ".msh" { $ftype = "MSH script" }
>>    ".txt" { $ftype = "Regular text file" }
>>    ".exe" { $ftype = "Executable file" }
>>    default { $ftype = "Unknown" }
>>}
>>$note=new-object System.Management.Automation.MshNoteProperty
"FriendlyType",$ftype
>>$_.MshObject.Properties.Add($note)
>>$_
>>}
>>
MSH D:\MshScripts> get-childitem | add-friendlytype | format-table
Name,FriendlyType
Name                               FriendlyType
----                               ------------
filter.msh                         MSH script
fn.msh                             MSH script
winword.exe                        Executable file
summary.txt                        Regular text file
outline.hxs                        Unknown
```

What Just Happened?

Filters are a special type of function intended to be used in a pipeline. Unlike functions, they do not block the pipeline, as there is no need to wait for $input to fill up with all of the incoming objects. The special variable $_ is prepopulated with the current pipeline object. Also, the script inside the filter has no knowledge of whether any objects have passed through the filter before the current one, nor whether any are due to follow it. This simplicity makes the task of writing a filter easier because it forces you to focus only on what to do with the object at hand.

It is usual, although not required, for a filter to put an object into the pipeline as an output. A filter that swallows every object it sees probably isn't going to be all that useful, especially if downstream processes are expecting objects to work with. It's totally legitimate for a filter to drop some or most objects that don't meet certain criteria, as we saw with the test-prime case. There's some overlap with a couple of cmdlets we've already covered. For example, a filter can be used to replicate the functionality of the where-object cmdlet; in this case, it allows only those FileInfo objects that have a certain extension:

```
filter where-executable { if ($_.Extension -eq ".msh") { $_ } }
```

In many simple cases, the where-object and foreach-object cmdlets are sufficient and eliminate the need to first define a filter and then include it in the pipeline sequence. However, there are no strict rules about when to use a filter and when to use where and foreach; for a given case, the where-object approach might be quicker, whereas in other cases, a parameters filter could make a compact and more readable pipeline.

One other feature we caught a glimpse of here is the note. Notes are a handy companion to use within a filter because they allow us to annotate objects with extra information as they pass through the pipeline. The same objects come out the other end of the filter, and downstream stages in the pipeline work, oblivious to its presence, unless they specifically look up its value. The code for adding a new note looks a little cumbersome here, but when taken on its own is just two lines:

```
$note = new-object System.Management.MshNoteProperty <note name>,<note
value>
<object to add note to>.MshObject.Properties.Add($note)
```

What About...

...That IIS logfile example? First of all, we'll use a new cmdlet, get-content, which reads a file and puts it into the pipeline line by line. Because some logfiles have comment lines, we'll pass each line through where-object to remove any lines that start with a pound sign (#). We'll also use a method of the String class, Split, to break out each space-separated part of the logfile line. When we're done, we'll be left with a hashtable containing the URLs that caused 404s and the number of times each URL appeared:

```
MSH D:\MshScripts> $badUrls=@{}
MSH D:\MshScripts> filter count-http404 {
>>$parts = $_.Split(" ")
>>if ($parts[10] -eq 404)
>>{
>>    $uri = $parts[4]
>>    if ($badUrls.Contains($uri)) { $badUrls[$uri]++ }
>>    else { $badUrls[$uri]=1 }
>>}
>>}
>>
MSH D:\MshScripts> get-content ex010101.log | where-object {$_ -notlike
"#*"} | count-http404
MSH D:\MshScripts> $badUrls
```

```
Key                 Value
---                 -----
/index.php            102
/robots.txt          1054
/cgi-bin/run.pl       320
/cgi-bin/exec.pl      993
/cmd.exe              821
/command.com         3822
```

This filter is fairly lightweight and simple at this point. With some creative use of the other data in the $parts array, it shouldn't take much extra effort to report on other aspects of the logfiles. Another route for expansion would be to consider passing wildcard filenames—for example, get-content ex0504??.log | ... to report on a whole month.

What's Next?

Now that we've spent time discussing the basics, it's time to explore some of the other features offered by the shell—in particular, the environment MSH provides for running scripts. In the next chapter, we'll see more about variables and scoping, as well as how MSH treats wildcards in text matching, property selection, and filename completion throughout the shell.

## CHAPTER 4

Managing MSH Scope and State

So far, we've seen a number of different aspects of MSH, including the idea of cmdlets, pipelines, and the shell language of variables, functions, and filters. In this chapter, we'll look at the MSH infrastructure that brings all of these components together and allows them to work seamlessly with each other.

In the following pages, we'll look at some of the services that MSH provides. The material we'll cover here is applicable throughout the shell, and tools such as text matching and regular expressions will likely become an indispensable part of your toolkit.

Control Access to Variables and Functions

We've already touched on the idea that variables defined in functions might not always be accessible from other functions, scripts, or cmdlets. This limited visibility is known as *scoping*, and it is used by MSH to segregate data when several different script blocks and cmdlets are in play. It's important to realize that scoping doesn't offer privacy or security; instead, the ability to hide is used to simplify the authoring of scripts. As we'll see, this behavior comes in handy with more complicated scripts and tasks as it reduces the potential for these script fragments to interfere with each other.

In general, MSH controls scope automatically; scripts and functions often "just work" as a result. However, it's always wise to understand how scoping comes into play, especially in cases in which there's a need to do something differently.

Managing Complexity

Given that the *cmd.exe* shell has survived without globally scoped variables for a long time, it's fair to ask why scoping is needed. The key difference is the arrival of reusable logic, both in terms of script files and functions. Think about using a script or function written by a coworker or downloaded from the Web: without a thorough inspection, could you confidently identify the names of all the variables it used?

Scoping allows scripts and functions to be written such that they'll perform a particular task with better control over any dependencies or side effects. Consider a function that needs to use a variable when doing its processing, such as the add function used in "Capture Reusable Behavior in a Function" in Chapter 3. Had this variable been used for some other purpose before calling the function, the results could have been quite unpredictable. Scoping provides a certain reassurance that functions, filters, and scripts will do exactly what they're intended to do and nothing more.

How Do I Do That?

In interactive mode, we are working in the *global* scope, in which any variables or functions defined are accessible from everywhere within the shell:

```
MSH D:\MshScripts> function showA { write-host $a }
MSH D:\MshScripts> $a = 10
MSH D:\MshScripts> showA
10
```

This little example seems obvious. Let's see what happens when we define a variable and assign it a value inside a function:

```
MSH D:\MshScripts> function doWork { $processes = get-process }
MSH D:\MshScripts> doWork
MSH D:\MshScripts> $processes.Count
MSH D:\MshScripts>
```

After we've run the function, it might be reasonable to expect that $processes would contain some data, yet it remains undefined when we try to inspect it. This is actually a good thing: If $processes had been storing important data, its value would have been accidentally overwritten inside the function call.

In fact, what we've done here is define a variable in a *local* scope (one that is created just for the function). By the time we're back at the prompt, any variables defined in that scope have disappeared. Generally speaking, this behavior helps functions keep their own activities to themselves and encourages information to be emitted explicitly as a result (as we saw in the previous chapter), rather than relying on variables to pass information around.

Because there are cases where we'd like variables to live longer than the lifetime of the function that defines them, MSH has syntax for working explicitly with variables in the global scope:

```
MSH D:\MshScripts> function doWork { $global:processes = get-process }
MSH D:\MshScripts> doWork
MSH D:\MshScripts> $processes.Count
29
```

This difference in scope can give rise to some unexpected behavior. In these cases, it's possible for a variable to take on a value that we don't expect or for an assignment to apparently fail. Let's go back to the showA example and add another function that updates the value of $a before we display it:

```
MSH D:\MshScripts> function setA { $a = 5 }
MSH D:\MshScripts> $a=10
MSH D:\MshScripts> setA
MSH D:\MshScripts> showA
10
```

As in the doWork example, here the setA function is making a change to its own $a variable in its local scope. Even though there's a global variable $a already present, the setA function will not make any changes to it. Because showA has a completely different local scope—one in which no local $a is present—it uses the value of the global $a instead.

Fortunately, MSH provides multiple levels of scope. When one function is invoked from inside another, the invoked function can see the global scope and the scope of its parent; it also has its own separate local scope. If we call the showA function from within a scope in which the value has been changed, it will see the new value instead:

```
MSH D:\MshScripts> function setAndShowA { $a = 5; showA }
MSH D:\MshScripts> $a=10
MSH D:\MshScripts> setAndShowA
5
MSH D:\MshScripts> $a
10
```

MSH offers several other explicit scope indictors in the same format as the global: syntax. As the local scope is always assumed, the following example is functionally equivalent to the previous setA definition, but the use of local: helps to convey the scope considerations (in other words, it clarifies how futile this setA function is):

```
MSH D:\MshScripts> function setA { $local:a = 5 }
```

Scripts, like functions, are run within their own special *script* scope, which is created when the script starts and discarded when it ends. The `script:` prefix is convenient for modifying variables that are defined in a script but that are outside of the current function and are not global variables. For example, consider a script similar to the one in Example 4-1 that keeps a tally of failures during a series of checks and reports the number of problems at the end of the script.

Example 4-1. Use of script scope variables in a script

```
function checkProcessCount
{
    if ((get-process).Count -gt 50)
    {
        $script:failureCount++
    }
}

$failureCount = 0
checkProcessCount
...
"Script complete with $failureCount errors"
```

In cases such as running the profile, we don't want a script to run in its own scope and would prefer it to impact the global scope. Instead of running the script by filename alone, it is *dot sourced* with a period followed by the filename. Running a script in this way tells MSH to load the child scope into the parent scope when the script is complete (see Example 4-2).

Example 4-2. DotSourceExample.msh

```
$c = 20
```

Now, we can see the difference between the two methods of running the script:

```
MSH D:\MshScripts> .\DotSourceExample.msh
MSH D:\MshScripts> $c

MSH D:\MshScripts> . .\DotSourceExample.msh
MSH D:\MshScripts> $c
20
```

What Just Happened?

Scoping applies to all user-defined elements of the MSH language, including variables, functions, and filters. Fortunately, it follows a series of simple rules and is always predictable.

There are four categories of scope: global, local, script, and private.

Global scope

Only one global scope is created per MSH session when the shell is started. Global scopes are not shared between different instances of MSH.

Local scope

A new local scope is always created when a function, filter, or script is run. The new scope has read access to all scopes of its parent, its parent's parent, and so on, up to the global scope. Because scopes are inherited downward in this fashion, children can read from (but not write to) the scope of their parents, yet parents cannot read from the scope of their children.

An alternative way of looking at this is to appreciate the lifetime of a scope (the time from its creation to the point at which it is discarded). Just as new scopes are created when entering a script block (or function, filter, etc.), they are discarded as soon as the script block is finished. Were a parent to try and access variables in a child's scope before the script block had run, the variables wouldn't exist yet; should they try afterward, the scope would have been discarded and all variables within it would be gone.

Script scope

A script scope is created whenever a script file is run, and it is discarded when the script finishes. All script files are subject to this behavior unless they are dot sourced, in which case their script scope is loaded into the scope of their parent when the script is complete. If one dot-sourced script (*a.msh*) dot sources another (*b.msh*), the same rules apply: when *b.msh* completes, its scope is loaded into the script scope of *a.msh*; when *a.msh* completes, their combined scopes are loaded into the parent scope.

Private scope

The private and local scopes are very similar, but they have one key difference: definitions made in the private scope are not inherited by any children scopes.

Table 4-1 summarizes the available scopes and their lifetimes.

Table 4-1. Scopes and their lifetimes

Scope name	Lifetime
Global	Entire MSH session
Local	Current script block and any scripts/functions invoked from it
Script	Current script file and any scripts/functions invoked from it
Private	Current script block only; scripts/functions invoked from current block will not inherit variables defined in this scope

There are a few general rules about scoping that are useful to remember:

- Unless explicitly stated, a variable can be read and changed only within the scope in which it was created.
- Scopes are inherited from parent to children. Children can access any data in their parents' scope with the exception of privately scoped variables.
- The local scope is always the current one, and any references are assumed to refer to it. In other words, any reference such as $a is interpreted as $local:a.
- The global, local, and private scopes are always available. In some cases, such as when working interactively at the prompt, the global and local scopes will be the same.

What About...

...What if I don't want functions to inherit the scope of the block that calls them? Although rarely used, this is the primary function of the *private* scope, which can be used to hide data from children. Working with the earlier example, if we now define $a as a private variable, subsequent function calls will be unable to retrieve its value:

```
MSH D:\MshScripts> $private:a = 5
MSH D:\MshScripts> showA
MSH D:\MshScripts>
```

...How does get-childitem Variable: deal with different scopes? As we've already seen, this special drive shows the variables defined for the current scope. Executing get-childitem Variable: from the prompt will show the content of the global scope. However, running the same command from within a script file or function may return a different list of results that will include all of the global variables plus any others than have been defined in the local scope.

Now, we're going to put variables aside for a while and discuss how the hosting environment handles strings of text.

Work with Special Characters

Although MSH does a good job of taking input and parsing it to get an understanding of intent, there are times when it needs some help. For example, consider the simple copy-item cmdlet, which takes two parameters: source and destination. In the typical case, usage is very simple and easy to follow:

```
MSH D:\MshScripts> copy-item file1 file2
```

But what happens when filenames contain spaces?

```
MSH D:\MshScripts> copy-item my file1 file2
```

Does this mean copy `my file1` to `file2`, copy `my` to `file1 file2`, or something else? Clearly, we need some way of identifying where one parameter ends and another begins. These quoting rules go beyond cmdlet parameters and are used consistently throughout the shell.

Next, we'll look at some of the different types of strings available, their delimiters, and some special character sequences employed by MSH that allow us to express exactly what we mean.

How Do I Do That?

Let's start with an easy example:

```
MSH D:\MshScripts> "In double quotes"
In double quotes
MSH D:\MshScripts> 'In single quotes'
In single quotes
```

Does this mean we can use single quotes and double quotes interchangeably? Not exactly. MSH makes a subtle but important distinction between the two: single quotes are used to represent a *literal* string (one that will be used exactly as is) whereas MSH looks through strings inside double quotes and replaces any variable names with their values in a process known as *variable expansion*:

```
MSH D:\MshScripts> $myName = "Andy"
MSH D:\MshScripts> "Hello, $myName"
Hello, Andy
MSH D:\MshScripts> 'Hello, $myName'
Hello, $myName
```

Single quotes are allowed inside of strings enclosed in double quotes and vice versa. This is often convenient when quotation marks are needed within a string.

```
MSH D:\MshScripts> $myName = "Andy"
MSH D:\MshScripts> 'He said "Hello, $myName"'
He said "Hello, $myName"
MSH D:\MshScripts> "He said 'Hello, $myName'"
He said 'Hello, Andy'
```

What if I really wanted to output He said "Hello, Andy" with double quotes instead? Nested quotation marks aren't going to cut it here, so we somehow need to include the double quote character inside the string.

MSH enables us to do this by *escaping* the double quote character, giving special instructions on how to interpret it differently than usual. When the grave accent character (`), also known as a backquote or backtick, is used inside a string, MSH understands that the character immediately following it has a special meaning.

```
MSH D:\MshScripts> "He said `"Hello, $myName`""
He said "Hello, Andy"
MSH D:\MshScripts> "Col 1`tCol 2`tCol 3"
Col 1    Col 2    Col 3
```

What Just Happened?

Because a string can be defined in MSH in different ways, the quoting rules are used to instruct the shell exactly how it should work with the content between the quotation marks and whether it should be passed straight through or undergo some processing first. The difference between the two main cases is in how MSH treats the $ sign and any variable names that follow it. If the single quotation marks are used, MSH does not inspect the string and uses it as is. By using double quotation marks, you are implicitly asking the shell to do a search on any variable names within the string, replacing them with the current value of the variable.

Variable expansion in double-quoted strings consistently follows some simple rules. If the $ sign appears in the string, any legal characters following it are assumed to refer to a variable name. MSH will look forward until it hits something that doesn't qualify (such as a space, newline, tab, comma, etc.) and use everything up to that point as the variable name. The shell then looks up the value of that variable, converts it to a string, and places the value into the original string:

```
MSH D:\MshScripts> $alpha = 2
MSH D:\MshScripts> $alphabet = 9
MSH D:\MshScripts> "$alphabet"
9                  # matches $alphabet not $alpha, otherwise this would
                   # return "2bet"
MSH D:\MshScripts> "some value=$undefinedVariableName"
some value=
```

Because MSH looks forward until it hits a nonalphanumeric character, a special syntax is used for the expansion of more complex variables such as arrays and hashtables. Parentheses can be used immediately after the $ sign to enclose the entire variable name and any indexers necessary for correct evaluation:

```
MSH D:\MshScripts> $arr = @("first","second")
MSH D:\MshScripts> "$arr[0]"
first second[0]           # Oops!
MSH D:\MshScripts> "$($arr[0])"
first
```

The ability to nest different styles of quotation marks inside each other is often a handy shortcut, but it is not a universal solution. For example, the string 'He said "I'm here"' is invalid because there is an uneven number of single quotation marks in the string. In anything but simple cases, it's better to rely on escape characters for including quotation marks inside a string.

With both of the approaches available, should single or double quotes be used? This depends on several factors. In clear-cut cases, the decision is based on the rules: if the string contains a $ sign that needs to be expanded, use double quotes; if the $ sign is intended literally, single quotes can be used or the character can be escaped as `$. In the general case, however, it often comes down to personal preference. Most of the examples we've seen throughout the book so far have used double quotes, even when variable expansion is not expected. This makes it very easy to add a variable into a string at a later date and have it expanded automatically with a negligible difference in performance.

The escape character (`) has a number of meanings depending on its location and usage. When used on the command line, it indicates that the character immediately following it should be passed on without substitution or processing, which is helpful when a character has meaning to MSH but isn't meant to be used in that fashion. For example:

```
MSH D:\MshScripts> write-host Use the -Object option
write-host : A parameter cannot be found that matches parameter 'Use'.
At line:1 char:11
+ write-host  <<<< Use the -Object option
MSH D:\MshScripts> write-host Use the `-Object option
Use the -Object option
MSH D:\MshScripts> copy-item my` file1 file2
# equivalent to copy "my file1" "file2"
```

When used within a string (of either single or double quote variety), MSH knows to replace the escape character and the character immediately following it with a special character. Table 4-2 lists some of the escape sequences you're likely to need.

Table 4-2. Common MSH escape sequences

Character	Meaning
`'	Single quote
`"	Double quote
``	Grave accent
`$	Dollar symbol
`0	Null character (different than $( ))

Table 4-2. Common MSH escape sequences (continued)

Character	Meaning
`a	Alert (beep)
`b	Backspace
`f	Form feed
`n	Newline
`r	Carriage return
`t	Tab
`v	Vertical tab

What About...

...Do Unix shells use the grave accent character for something else? Yes. In many shells, the grave accent character is used for command substitution when the output of a command is assigned to a variable and used for further processing.

For example, in bash:

```
PROCESSOR=`uname -p`
NOW=`date`
echo "This machine is a $PROCESSOR"
echo "Current time is $NOW"
```

Command substitution is a critical tool when data is passed around as text without any definition of structure. Because MSH works more comfortably with structured data, it's usually more convenient to draw information from the shell, another cmdlet, or the .NET Framework than it is to draw information from the textual output of another command.

The equivalent MSH script would read:

```
$processor = $Env:PROCESSOR_IDENTIFIER
$now = get-date
write-host "This machine is a $processor"
write-host "Current time is $now"
```

Of course, given that $processor and $now represent structured data, we're in a position to work with information such as $now.Year without any further effort. In any case, the direct equivalent to the `...` syntax is $(...), which will cause MSH to evaluate the expression in parentheses (e.g., "The current date is $(get-date)").

...What about "here strings"? The term *here string* refers to a third technique for defining strings. Two markers are used to represent the start and end of the string (@" and "@, respectively), and anything that stands between them, including newline characters, is included in the definition:

```
MSH D:\MshScripts> $a = 10
MSH D:\MshScripts> $longString = @"
>>First line
>>Second line
>>Variable expansion $a
>>"@
>>
MSH D:\MshScripts> $longString
First line
Second line
Variable expansion 10
MSH D:\MshScripts>
```

MSH does provide equivalent command substitution syntax for cases in which it is necessary to capture the textual output of a command:

```
$pingTarget="127.0.0.1"
$pingOutput = $(ping $pingTarget)
```

Use Wildcards to Define a Set of Items

Wildcard matching is one of the great shortcuts provided by almost all command shells available today. Instead of having to enumerate a list of files one by one, we can use some special characters that translate to "anything." In this section, we'll look at some of the evolutionary changes in MSH with regard to wildcard matching, and we'll see how some of the new syntax can be used to list sets of files for processing more easily.

How Do I Do That?

When it comes to wildcards, MSH supports the familiar wildcard syntax using the ? and * characters to represent any character and any sequence of characters, respectively. For a quick refresher, let's look at a few commands that make use of these wildcard characters:

```
MSH D:\MshScripts> get-childitem *.msh


    Directory: FileSystem::D:\MshScripts


Mode    LastWriteTime     Length Name
----    -------------     ------ ----
-a---   Mar 20 21:55        491  createfiles.msh
-a---   Mar 20 18:15        118  updatefiles.msh
-a---   Mar 23 00:50        117  unittest1.msh
-a---   Mar 28 22:04        243  unittest2.msh
```

```
-a---    Mar 22 23:36        49  unittest4.msh
-a---    Mar 22 23:36        88  unittestA.msh


MSH D:\MshScripts> get-childitem *files.msh


    Directory: FileSystem::D:\MshScripts


Mode    LastWriteTime        Length Name
----    -------------        ------ ----
-a---    Mar 20 21:55        491  createfiles.msh
-a---    Mar 20 18:15        118  updatefiles.msh

MSH D:\MshScripts> get-childitem unittest?.msh


    Directory: FileSystem::D:\MshScripts


Mode    LastWriteTime        Length Name
----    -------------        ------ ----
-a---    Mar 23 00:50        117  unittest1.msh
-a---    Mar 28 22:04        243  unittest2.msh
-a---    Mar 22 23:36        49  unittest4.msh
```

MSH offers several other wildcard characters for more flexibility in wildcard matching. Square brackets ([ ]) can be used to specify a set of characters, any one of which can be used to make a match. In other words, square brackets behave somewhat like the question mark (?) but, instead of matching any character, they match just those characters that appear inside the brackets. Sometimes, instead of having to write out every possible character, it's more convenient to define a range; the hyphen character (-) can be used between a start and an end character to indicate that anything in between is also valid:

```
MSH D:\MshScripts> get-childitem unittest[14].msh


    Directory: FileSystem::D:\MshScripts


Mode    LastWriteTime        Length Name
----    -------------        ------ ----
-a---    Mar 23 00:50        117  unittest1.msh
-a---    Mar 22 23:36        49  unittest4.msh

MSH D:\MshScripts> get-childitem unittest[a-z].msh


    Directory: FileSystem::D:\MshScripts
```

```
Mode     LastWriteTime      Length Name
----     -------------      ------ ----
-a---    Mar 22 23:36          88  unittestA.msh
```

What About…

…Using a wildcard character in your filenames? Although most common filesystems prohibit the use of the ? and * in file and folder names, the [and] characters are generally available. If you have a file called *default[12].htm*, the command get-childitem default[12].htm won't find it because the wildcard rules tell the cmdlet to look for *default1.htm* and *default2.htm*. In this case, the escape character can be used to tell MSH not to expand the wildcard syntax; get-childitem default`[12`].htm will work well.

Where Can I Learn More?

The help page for the topic about_Wildcard contains more information about the changes in wildcard matches and introduces a couple of other special match characters, including ^ and $, which refer to the start and end of the filename, respectively.

With this flexibility at our fingertips when matching against filenames, it seems unjust that so far we've only been able to use the -eq comparison operator to test whether two strings are identical. It's time to see how wildcards can be applied to text strings in comparisons.

Take String Comparison Beyond -eq, -lt, and -gt

In Chapter 3, we looked at a number of comparison operators, such as -eq, -lt, and -gt, which can be applied to many of the different types of data we work with in the shell. Each of these three operators works effectively on strings by checking for identical strings and giving some idea of relative alphabetical ordering. However, there are many cases in which we'd like to do a more meaningful comparison of the actual letters within a string—for example, to test whether the string contains a certain shorter string or whether it matches a certain format such as the aaa.bbb.ccc.ddd format of a numeric IP address.

We'll look at two approaches to matching strings in this section. The first case uses the -like operator with some basic wildcard rules to see whether one string contains another. The second technique uses the -match operator and relies on regular expressions to communicate more complex matching rules. Before we begin, let's look at some examples of regular expressions.

Fear of Regular Expressions

Regular expressions can appear very daunting at first glance. The seemingly senseless sequence of backslashes, characters, parentheses, brackets, and other punctuation can easily become overwhelming. Authoring regular expressions isn't necessarily a skill you can pick up overnight, nor should you need to. Careful use of the -match operator with some well-crafted regular expressions is a handy way to match text quickly and efficiently. However, if you find yourself authoring regular expressions that are hundreds of characters long, it may be time to think about breaking the tests out separately and perhaps grouping them together inside a function.

Regular Expressions

A *regular expression* describes a set of matching strings according to a series of rules. In this section, we'll cover a few of the basic rules and look at some common examples, but it's important to realize that regular expressions are a vast topic that won't be covered exhaustively here. For a more complete picture of the topic, consider picking up a copy of *Mastering Regular Expressions* (O'Reilly).

There are three principles that are fundamental to understanding and effectively using regular expressions. The first is the concept of alternates—that is, the idea that a single regular expression can express two or more different strings to match against. Alternates are separated by a vertical bar (|), which is the same symbol used for building a pipeline. For example, the regular expression w3svc|iisadmin|msftpsvc matches "w3svc", "iisadmin", "msftpsvc", and the string "w3svc service is started but iisadmin is not." Square brackets are often used as shorthand for specifying single-character alternates—for example, where [aeiou] is equivalent to a|e|i|o|u. The hyphen can also be used inside brackets to cover a range; [a-m] matches any letter in the first half of the alphabet.

Second, different parts of a regular expression can be grouped together using parentheses. Grouping is useful when only part of a longer regular expression is subject to alternation or quantification. For example, the regular expression (w3|msftp)svc matches both "w3svc" and "msftpsvc." Groups can be nested inside each other, provided every open parenthesis is matched to a closing one.

Quantification, the third key part of regular expressions, gives us the power to specify how many times a certain character or sequence must occur to constitute a match. For example, the regular expression (domain\\)?user would match "user" and "domain\user" but not "domain\domain\user". Table 4-3 describes the quantifiers available for use.

Table 4-3. Common quantifiers for denoting quantity in regular expressions

Quantifier	Matches the preceding expression…
*	Zero or more times
+	One or more times
?	Once at most
{n}	Exactly n times
{n,}	At least n times
{n,m}	At least n and at most m times

Regular expressions can also use a set of special characters as shorthand for common matches. These special characters, shown in Table 4-4, are different from those covered earlier in this chapter, and they apply only to regular expressions.

Table 4-4. Common special characters used in regular expressions

Special character	Meaning
.	Any single character
^	Start of a string
$	End of a string
\b	Word boundary (such as a space or newline)
\d	Digit (0–9)
\n	Newline
\s	Whitespace (space, tab, newline, etc.)
\t	Tab
\w	Word (alphabet plus digits and underscore)

Many of these special characters have an inverse associated with their capital letter form. For example, \S matches anything that isn't whitespace, and \W matches anything that isn't a word or digit.

To wrap up this short tour, Table 4-5 contains a few examples of simple regular expressions that we'll rely on in the examples that follow.

Table 4-5. Simple regular expressions

Type of information	Regular expression
Windows username	`(\w*\\)?\w*`
IP address	`^\d+\.\d+\.\d+\.\d+$`
Simple private IP addresses (RFC 1918 defined 10.x.x.x, 172.16-32.x.x, 192.168.x.x)	`^(10\.\d+\.\d+\.\d+|172\.[1-3][0-9]\.\d+\.\d+|192\.168\.\d+\.\d+)$`
GUID (in the registry format of {xxxxxxxx-xxxx-xxxx-xxxx-xxxxxxxxxxxx})	`^{?[0-9a-f]{8}-([0-9a-f]{4}-){3}[0-9a-f]{12}}?$`

With the basics in place, it's time to match some strings.

How Do I Do That?

Let's start by reviewing the -eq comparison operator. When used on strings, -eq does a case-insensitive test to see whether strings are identical—not close, but identical:

```
MSH D:\MshScripts> "foo" -eq "foo"
True
MSH D:\MshScripts> "foo" -eq "bar"
False
MSH D:\MshScripts> "foo " -eq "foo"
False
MSH D:\MshScripts> "foo" -eq "FOO"
True
```

The -like operator brings into play all of the wildcards we just saw. The behaviors of *, ?, [, and] all follow the same rules as we saw when matching filenames:

```
MSH D:\MshScripts> "foo" -like "foo"
True
MSH D:\MshScripts> "foobar" -like "foo*"
True
MSH D:\MshScripts> "foobar" -like "*ba?"
True
MSH D:\MshScripts> "gray" -like "gr[ae]y"
True
```

-like has a related operator, -clike, that is used to perform case-sensitive matching. The two operators treat wildcards in almost exactly the same fashion; the only difference is that the -clike operator distinguishes between uppercase and lowercase letters:

```
MSH D:\MshScripts> "foo" -like "FOO"
True
MSH D:\MshScripts> "foo" -clike "FOO"
False
```

Both -like and -clike have inverse commands that return true when no match is made and false when a match is present. The -notlike operator is a handy shortcut for -not ("a" -like "b"):

```
MSH D:\MshScripts> "foo" -notlike "FOO"
False
MSH D:\MshScripts> "foo" -cnotlike "FOO"
True
```

Wildcard comparisons are a useful tool and can be applied to all types of string-matching tasks. However, there are types of strings that cannot be captured in sufficient detail with wildcards alone. For example, it's possible to match one character (?) or any number of characters (*), yet there's no way to express a match of, say, exactly four. Likewise, a wildcard match is wide open—letters, numbers, and punctuation are all allowed. For some more specific matches, it's time to bring in the regular expressions.

MSH performs regular expression matching with the -match operator. As with -like, it, too, has related operators for case sensitivity (-cmatch) and negative matches (-notmatch and -cnotmatch).

Let's look at a few simple regular expression matches. Although we're looking at all of these examples as simple command-line Boolean tests, these ideas can easily be transferred to other places, such as the where-object cmdlet, taking wildcards to a whole new level:

```
MSH C:\WINDOWS\system32> "ipv6.exe" -match ".*exe"
True
MSH D:\MshScripts> "ipv6.exe" -match ".*\d{1}.*exe"
True
MSH D:\MshScripts> "ipv6.exe" -match ".*\d{2}.*exe"
False                    # regex required two consecutive digits
MSH D:\MshScripts> get-childitem | where-object { $_ -match ".*\d{2}.*exe" }


    Directory: FileSystem::C:\WINDOWS\System32


Mode                LastWriteTime     Length Name
----                -------------     ------ ----
-a---        8/4/2004     5:00 AM      47104 cmdl32.exe
-a---        8/4/2004     5:00 AM      39936 cmmon32.exe
-a---        8/4/2004     5:00 AM      45568 drwtsn32.exe
-a---        8/4/2004     5:00 AM      45568 extrac32.exe
-a---        8/4/2004     5:00 AM      92224 krnl386.exe
-a---        8/4/2004     5:00 AM     123392 mplay32.exe
-a---        8/4/2004     5:00 AM       3252 nw16.exe
-a---        8/4/2004     5:00 AM      32768 odbcad32.exe
-a---        8/4/2004     5:00 AM       3584 regedt32.exe
-a---        8/4/2004     5:00 AM      11776 regsvr32.exe
-a---        8/4/2004     5:00 AM      33280 rundll32.exe
...
```

It's worthwhile to compare the behavior of -like with -match to better understand their differences. Even the simplest cases turn up some surprises:

```
MSH D:\MshScripts> "foobar" -like "foo"
False
MSH D:\MshScripts> "foobar" -match "foo"
True
```

When used without any special characters, quantifiers, or alternates, regular expression matching is similar to wildcard matching with one key difference: if no wildcards are present in a -like match, the strings must be identical for a match to occur, whereas with a regular expression, it's sufficient for the string to simply contain the regular expression. When writing regular expressions, it's important to keep this in mind and start the regular expression with a caret (^) and end it with a dollar sign ($). The following example shows the different outcomes that result when you try to match an invalid dotted IP address against the two types of regular expression:

```
MSH D:\MshScripts> "1.2.3.4.5" -match "\d+\.\d+\.\d+\.\d+"
True          # No!
MSH D:\MshScripts> "1.2.3.4.5" -match "^\d+\.\d+\.\d+\.\d+$"
False         # That's better
```

Let's take a look at a slightly more involved example. First, we'll use the regular expression for a GUID and verify that it's working correctly against a sample GUID:

```
MSH D:\MshScripts> $guidRegex = "^{?[0-9a-f]{8}-([0-9a-f]{4}-){3}
[0-9a-f]{12}}?$"
MSH D:\MshScripts> $myGuid = [System.Guid]::NewGuid().ToString()
MSH D:\MshScripts> $myGuid
496a3bc7-861d-4176-9778-e01f266ba835
MSH D:\MshScripts> $myGuid -match $guidRegex
True
```

For one last example, let's turn our attention to IP addresses. To grab the current IP address, we'll again dip into the .NET Framework and then run the IP through a couple of regular expressions to confirm that it's both valid and non-private:

```
MSH D:\MshScripts> function get-ipaddress {
>>$hostname = [System.Net.Dns]::GetHostName()
>>$hosts = [System.Net.Dns]::GetHostByName($hostname)
>>$hosts.AddressList[0].ToString()
>>}
>>
MSH D:\MshScripts> $ipRegex = "^\d+\.\d+\.\d+\.\d+$"
MSH D:\MshScripts> $privateIpRegex = "^(10\.\d+\.\d+\.\d+|172\.[1-3][0-9]\.\
d+\.\d+|192\.168\.\d+\.\d+)$"
MSH D:\MshScripts> $myIP = get-ipaddress
MSH D:\MshScripts> $myIP
169.254.136.191
```

```
MSH D:\MshScripts> $myIP -match $ipRegex
True
MSH D:\MshScripts> $myIP -notmatch $privateIpRegex
True
```

What About...

...Why is -like needed? Can't its behavior be achieved just by using the -match operator? While it's true that regular expressions can be used to get the same results as wildcard matches, there are good reasons to have both. If the -like wildcard syntax makes a comparison easier to read, it usually makes long-term maintenance of scripts easier as well.

...Does variable expansion work here? Absolutely. As we saw earlier, MSH exercises variable expansion on any strings it sees that are enclosed in double quotes. Make sure to use single or double quotes appropriately, depending on how you want MSH to handle your variables:

```
MSH D:\MshScripts> $myVar = "Andy"
MSH D:\MshScripts> "Hello, $myVar" -ilike "*andy*"
True
MSH D:\MshScripts> $myRegex = "\d{3}"
MSH D:\MshScripts> "test133" -match "test$myRegex"
True
MSH D:\MshScripts> "test148" -match 'test$myRegex'   # no expansion
False
```

Where Can I Learn More?

We've only scratched the surface of regular expressions in this section. They stand as a very expressive tool for solving all types of text-matching scenarios, and they can be significantly more complex and powerful than the examples we've looked at here. The regular expression language covered here is precisely the same as the one offerered by the .NET Framework. Information is available at *http://msdn.microsoft.com/library/default.asp?url=/library/en-us/cpgenref/html/cpconregularexpressionslanguageelements.asp*.

We've covered a number of distinct aspects of the MSH infrastructure in this chapter. We'll wrap up with a discussion of the error-handling mechanisms built into MSH.

When Things Go Wrong

For anything but the simplest of tasks, there's always a chance that something can go wrong. Aware that processes and scripts don't always run as planned and can sometimes hit unexpected problems, MSH offers an error-handling system that gives the script author the ability to control what happens next in times of trouble.

Before we begin, it's important to call out the two types of errors that can occur when processing a command. The first type, a *non-terminating error*, indicates that some problem has occurred but that execution can still continue. An example of a non-terminating error is an access problem that occurs when trying to read a protected resource or write to a read-only file. In contrast, a *terminating error* signifies a condition in which execution cannot possibly continue and the command is terminated.

The core of the error-handling system is exposed by the trap keyword. The keyword is always followed by a script block that contains instructions for what to do when an error occurs. To make use of this, we'll also come across some additional ubiquitous parameters that are used to specify what a cmdlet should do in the case of error.

How Do I Do That?

Let's start with a simple example that is guaranteed to cause a problem: division by zero. Dividing any number by zero generates an error message and causes MSH to complain:

```
MSH D:\MshScripts> 100/0
Attempted to divide by zero.
At line:1 char:5
+ 100/0 <<<<
```

Whenever a runtime error occurs, MSH automatically updates the special $error array with information about the problem. The most recent error is in the first slot ([0]), the second most recent at [1], and so on:

```
MSH D:\MshScripts> $error[0]
Attempted to divide by zero.
```

The $error variable is useful for diagnosing errors after execution has finished, but suppose we'd like to take action as the problems arise. For this simple example, instead of just writing out the message to the screen, we want to write out a special message when a problem occurs. Let's create a script, shown in Example 4-3, that contains a very simple error handler.

Example 4-3. SimpleTrap.msh

```
trap
{
    "In error handler"
}

100/0
```

Now, when we run the script, we'll see that our own trap statement is run. This is just the beginning:

```
MSH D:\MshScripts> SimpleTrap.msh
In error handler
: Attempted to divide by zero.
At D:\MshScripts\SimpleTrap.msh:6 char:5
+ 100/0 <<<<
```

When inside the trap block, MSH automatically populates the special variable $_ with details of the problem that landed execution there. Now we're in business. Example 4-4 contains the improved trap handler.

Example 4-4. ImprovedTrap.msh

```
trap
{
    "In error handler"
    "Problem:"+$_.Message
}

100/0
```

Dealing with division by zero cases probably isn't typical of day-to-day problems. Let's instead look at the task of copying a set of files where we know one will fail. For this scenario, let's assume we have one folder, *source*, that contains files *a.txt*, *b.txt*, and *c.txt*, and we're planning to copy them into the dest folder that already contains a write-protected copy of *a.txt*. We can set up this little structure from either an MSH or CMD prompt with the following commands:

```
mkdir source
"content" > source\a.txt
"content" > source\b.txt
"content" > source\c.txt

mkdir dest
copy source\a.txt dest\a.txt
attrib +r dest\a.txt
```

Now that we're set up, let's try copying the contents of *source* to *dest*:

```
MSH D:\MshScripts> copy-item source\* dest
copy-item : Access to the path 'D:\MshScripts\dest\a.txt' is denied.
```

As expected, we see that the *a.txt* file could not be overwritten because it is write-protected. However, on closer inspection, look what made it into *dest*:

```
MSH D:\MshScripts> get-childitem dest


    Directory: FileSystem::D:\MshScripts\dest
```

```
Mode      LastWriteTime     Length Name
----      -------------     ------ ----
-ar--     Apr 05 16:16           9 a.txt
-a---     Apr 05 16:16           9 b.txt
-a---     Apr 05 16:16           9 c.txt
```

Sure enough, the *b.txt* and *c.txt* files made it over. Although the copy-item cmdlet hit a problem, it kept on trying to copy the other files that matched the wildcard.

The cmdlet's behavior in the face of a non-terminating error is controlled by the -ErrorAction option. By default, this takes a value of Continue, which, in case you hadn't guessed, instructs the cmdlet to notify the user that a problem occurred (by generating the "Access to the path..." message in this case) and continue processing any additional cases. By using another ErrorAction setting, we can change how the cmdlet deals with problems.

First, let's reset the scenario by deleting the *b.txt* and *c.txt* files with a del dest\[bc].txt command. This time, we'll tell MSH to ask us what to do if any problems arise by using the -ErrorAction Inquire setting:

```
MSH D:\MshScripts> copy-item –ErrorAction Inquire source\* dest

Confirm
Access to the path 'D:\MshScripts\dest\a.txt' is denied.
[Y] Yes  [A] Yes to All  [H] Halt Command  [S] Suspend  [?] Help
(default is "Y"):
```

MSH will now wait for some user input about what to do next before it moves ahead.

Finally, let's take a look at Stop, one of the other ErrorAction settings that effectively transforms any non-terminating errors into terminating errors and instructs the cmdlet to give up immediately and execute the trap handler if present. In Example 4-5, we bring together a handful of the techniques we've learned so far to create a simple script for ROBOCOPY-like behavior that will retry a file copy 10 times before giving up. For the sake of consistency, we'll continue to try overwriting the write-protected file so, it's fairly unlikely that any of the 10 attempts will succeed.

Example 1 5. RetryCopy.msh

```
$retryCount=10

while ($retryCount -gt 0)
{
        $success = $true
```

Example 4-5. RetryCopy.msh (continued)

```
    trap {
            $script:retryCount--
            $script:success = 0
            "Retrying.."
            continue
    }

    copy-item -ErrorAction Stop source\* dest

    if ($success) { $retryCount = 0 }
}

"Done"
```

When it comes time to run this script, we'll see the script iterating through its loop before finally giving up:

```
MSH D:\MshScripts> .\retryCopy.msh
Retrying..
Retrying..
Retrying..
Retrying..
Retrying..
Retrying..
Retrying..
Retrying..
Retrying..
Retrying..
Done
```

What Just Happened?

The trap keyword is a basic part of the MSH script language and is equal in standing to many other keywords such as while, if, and for. The trap keyword can be followed by an error type in square brackets to indicate that its handler should only be run if the error is of the specified type. For example, to catch only problems with division by zero, we would write the following:

```
trap [DivideByZeroException]
{
    "Divide by zero trapped"
    break
}
```

A trap must always include a script block, which defines the instructions to run when a problem arises. The $_ special variable is always available within the script block to enable the script to figure out what went wrong (which is often useful for deciding what to do next).

trap blocks are subject to scoping rules just as variables are. A trap block is entered only when an error occurs at that level. A parent scope will never invoke the trap handlers of any children, but an error inside a child (such as a function, filter, or loop) will cause execution to jump to the nearest trap block. Each scope can contain several trap blocks; when more than one is present, each is executed in turn when a problem arises.

After execution has finished inside the trap block, the error has usually become evident to the user. By placing a continue statement at the end of the trap block (as the last instruction before the closing brace), MSH understands that it is to continue at the end of the trap handler instead of terminating execution.

The ErrorAction option has a number of different settings that control how cmdlets behave when problems arise. In a pipeline, it's valid to use different ErrorAction settings for different stages; indeed, it's this fine-grain control that gives MSH its flexibility in handling different types of errors at each stage of processing. Table 4-6 describes the valid ErrorAction settings and the effects of each one.

Table 4-6. ErrorAction values and their effects

ErrorAction value	Effect
Stop	Abort on failure and treat all non-terminating errors as terminating
Continue	Generate an error and continue
Inquire	Ask the user how to proceed (see below)
SilentlyContinue	Proceed to the next item without generating an error

The Inquire prompt is worthy of a short discussion. It is shown when a problem arises and user input is needed to determine the next steps. The "Yes" option allows execution to start up again but will result in a similar prompt for every failure case that follows. Meanwhile, "Yes to All" assumes that "Yes" will be the answer for any future failures, so no further questions will be asked. "No" has the effect of stopping the cmdlet in its tracks so that no further processing will be attempted, whereas "No to All" is assumed to stop all future cmdlets. The "Suspend" option is useful because it starts a little sub-shell with all of the current settings, state, and an MSH> prompt, and it allows for browsing and troubleshooting. In the previous example, we could have used a sub-shell to run a quick attrib -r a.txt to resolve the issue.

What About...

...Changing the default `ErrorAction` value? Yes, you can do it. Instead of having to supply an `-ErrorAction` option for every cmdlet, MSH actually picks up the default value from a global variable called `$ErrorActionPreference`. If your preference is to have MSH ask how to proceed in every instance of a problem, add a `$ErrorActionPreference="Inquire"` line to your profile.

What's Next?

So far, we've made good progress and have covered all the basics of the MSH environment and its language features. In the next chapter, we'll spend some time focusing on the pipeline, examining its behavior in more depth, and looking at how we can really make use of the rich data that passes through it.

## CHAPTER 5

Adding to the MSH Toolkit

We covered a lot of new ground in the preceding chapters that focused on exploration in interactive mode. In the examples that follow in this chapter, we'll step back and look at some of the plumbing of MSH that makes it all possible. We'll cover some of the generic cmdlets in more detail, discuss how data can be persisted to and retrieved from a filesystem, and take a deeper look at exactly what a pipeline object is and how the .NET Framework Class Library can provide an extra dimension of functionality.

Extend the Toolkit with Generic Cmdlets

There are several cmdlets that keep coming up again and again: where-object, sort-object, select-object, format-table, and a handful of others. These cmdlets are simple in their design and offer almost limitless possibilities for reuse in all kinds of situations. There are several more processing cmdlets that we'll discuss in this section that are also generic in nature yet draw strength from their simplicity.

A Cmdlet for Every Occasion

As you begin to use MSH more, you'll quickly find yourself reaching for a handful of versatile cmdlets again and again. Depending on your usage patterns and tasks, you may find some more valuable than others. In any case, it's useful to remember that these cmdlets, no matter how infrequently used, are out there and waiting to be put into action.

For example, if you find yourself wondering why there isn't a cmdlet for calculating the average size of files in a directory, you might want to look again: a get-childitem and measure-object combo can probably achieve precisely those numbers with a minimum amount of effort.

How Do I Do That?

We've already covered the select-object cmdlet, so we can begin there. Previously, we saw a couple of its capabilities—for example, how it can create cut-down copies of incoming objects, and how it can take an object's property value and expand a collection into the pipeline. select-object has two additional command-line options, -first and -last, which instruct it to filter incoming objects passed solely on their sequence. This is similar to the head and tail commands found in other shells.

```
MSH C:\WINDOWS> get-childitem | select-object -first 10


    Directory: FileSystem::C:\WINDOWS


Mode     LastWriteTime       Length Name
----     -------------       ------ ----
-a---    Apr 24 16:04       1920054 BGInfo.bmp
-a---    Mar 25 04:00          1272 Blue Lace 16.bmp
-a--s    Apr 24 15:47          2048 bootstat.dat
-a---    Apr 24 15:15          4348 certocm.log
-a---    Mar 25 04:00         82944 clock.avi
-a---    Mar 25 04:00         17062 Coffee Bean.bmp
-a---    Apr 24 15:15         16012 comsetup.log
-a---    Apr 24 14:58             0 control.ini
-a---    Mar 25 04:00             2 desktop.ini
-a---    Mar 25 04:00         56832 dialer.exe


MSH C:\WINDOWS> get-childitem | select-object -last 10


    Directory: FileSystem::C:\WINDOWS


Mode     LastWriteTime       Length Name
----     -------------       ------ ----
d----    Apr 24 14:51                srchasst
d----    Apr 24 07:40                system
d----    Apr 24 19:05                system32
d----    Apr 24 07:40                TAPI
d---s    Apr 24 15:20                Tasks
d----    May 22 14:42                Temp
d----    Apr 24 07:32                twain_32
d----    Apr 24 15:42                VMADD
d-r--    Apr 24 14:53                Web
d----    Apr 24 15:56                WinSxS
```

`select-object` has another option that can be used to filter the pipeline such that only unique objects are returned. When dealing with large amounts of data, it's sometimes convenient to see just the range of values rather than the actual values. For example, a typical call to `get-service` will return nearly 100 services, each with its own name and status. If we're interested only in seeing the different values of service state in this list, the -unique option can help:

```
MSH D:\MshScripts> get-service | select-object Status -unique


                          Status
                          ------
                          Stopped
                          Running
```

This filtering of unique objects turns out to be quite useful. When the `select-object` -Unique cmdlet is placed in a pipeline, it will remove any duplicate objects. The first instance will be allowed to pass through, but any subsequent identical objects will be dropped:

```
MSH D:\MshScripts> "aa","aa","bb" | select-object -Unique
aa
bb
```

One other cmdlet that deserves a mention is `measure-object`. Think of this cmdlet as a universal tape measure; it can be used in any pipeline to give statistics about the objects that are moving through. When used without any options, it will just count the number of objects it sees. It becomes somewhat more interesting when the -Property option is used to measure a particular property of the incoming objects; when combined with some combination of the -Average, -Sum, -Min, and -Max options, `measure-object` will report some basic statistical analysis of the property:

```
MSH D:\MshScripts> get-childitem | measure-object


Count    : 18
Average  :
Sum      :
Max      :
Min      :
Property :

MSH D:\MshScripts> get-childitem | measure-object -Property Length -Average
-Sum -Min -Max
```

```
Count    : 18
Average  : 10492.1111111111
Sum      : 188858
Max      : 101546
Min      : 0
Property : Length
```

What About...

Can the commands head and tail be used instead of select-object and its
options? Yes, but since it's important to also pass a parameter to the cmdlet,
it is not possible to use an alias. Instead, functions can be used to call the
cmdlet with the right parameters. As a bonus, Example 5-1 can also take a
filename as a parameter, allowing usage like head longfile.txt –count 5.

Example 5-1. Simple head and tail functions

```
function head {
    param($filename, $count = 10)
    if ($filename) { $source = get-content $filename }
    else { $source = $input }
    $source | select-object –first $count
}

function tail {
    param($filename, $count = 10)
    if ($filename) { $source = get-content $filename }
    else { $source = $input }
    $source | select-object –last $count
}
```

De-duping simple arrays may not seem all that useful, but as we'll see in the
next section, there are cmdlets that can take a text file from disk and put it
into the pipeline line by line. Removing duplicate lines from a text file can be
a more meaningful task. For example, consider parsing IIS logfiles in much
the same way as we saw at the end of Chapter 3, except this time, let's do
away with the hashtable and list the unique set of successfully requested
URLs:

```
MSH D:\MshScripts> filter ExtractUrl { $parts = $_.Split(" "); if
($parts[10] -eq 200) { $parts[4] } }
MSH D:\MshScripts> get-content ex010101.log | ExtractUrl | select-object
-Unique
/default.aspx
/images/banner_bottom.gif
/images/banner_left.gif
/images/banner_right.gif
/images/banner_top.gif
/robots.txt
...
```

Where Can I Learn More?

Built-in help continues to be the ever-present reference point for cmdlet syntax and options. In particular, take a look at some of the other parameters available on the select-object and measure-object cmdlets: there's more functionality there than meets the eye.

Work with Text Files

We've already seen how scripts and functions can be captured in MSH script files and saved to disk for later use. Now, it's time to take a look at the results they produce and how those, too, can be persisted to a permanent store. Unlike most other shells, MSH works seamlessly with several different input and output formats, including simple text, comma-separated variable lists, and even XML representation: the data interchange format is no longer dictated by the toolset! We'll start by looking at data storage in text files and move on to other structured formats in the next section.

How Do I Do That?

get-content is a simple cmdlet that reads from the filesystem and puts each line of content (in the form of a string) into the pipeline in sequence. Its behavior is so similar to the type command in *cmd.exe* (and the cat command in Unix shells) that it is aliased with both terms by default. Both type and get-content can be used interchangeably in the examples that follow, but we'll use get-content for consistency. The first couple of examples use a simple text file that contains the familiar sentence "The quick brown fox jumped over the lazy dog," separated across three lines, as shown below:

```
MSH D:\MshScripts> get-content brownfox.txt
The quick brown fox
jumped over
the lazy dog
```

As we saw at the end of Chapter 3, it's convenient to pipe the output of get-content into other cmdlets. Let's revisit the versatile measure-object cmdlet, but this time, let's use some options that are designed precisely for sequences of lines such as those in a text file: -lines, -words, and -characters:

```
MSH D:\MshScripts> get-content brownfox.txt | measure-object -lines -words
-characters

Lines          Words          Characters      Property
-----          -----          ----------      --------
3              9              42
```

out-file is used to make changes to files stored on the filesystem. When given a filename, it will use the default formatter to output the contents of the pipeline to the filesystem:

```
MSH D:\MshScripts> get-process | out-file raw.txt
MSH D:\MshScripts> get-content raw.txt

Handles  NPM(K)    PM(K)      WS(K) VS(M)   CPU(s)     Id ProcessName
-------  ------    -----      ----- -----   ------     -- -----------
    672      12    11768      10956    65   184.73   1520 CcmExec
     24       1     1412       1440    13     0.04   3412 cmd
    462       5     1736       2156    25   114.71    352 csrss
    256       5     2428       7376    30    28.33   2932 dllhost
    433      15     8820      12076    64    90.73   2260 explorer
      0       0        0         16     0               0 Idle
...
```

What About...

...Controlling scrolling when a text file is too long to fit on a single screen? The MORE command in *cmd.exe* is used to page output, waiting for a key press at the end of each screen of information. This functionality is carried over into MSH in the form of a standard function. Feel free to put more at the end of the pipeline to pace the output: get-content longfile.txt | more.

Where Can I Learn More?

The get-help system has more details on the get-content and out-file cmdlets. For more information on using other data formats, keep reading.

Work with Structured File Formats

Text files are great for storing simple, human-readable information, but they're not ideally suited to representing the structured data that we're becoming accustomed to in MSH. More often than not, we're dealing with objects and properties rather than strings and characters. MSH supports an additional data format with ease: comma-separated variables (CSV).

With two additional cmdlets for working with comma-separated data, easy-to-use spreadsheet applications can be combined with the power of the shell. Whether used for input (managing a task list in a friendly interface) or output (such as drawing graphs and performing statistical analysis), the CSV format can be very useful.

How Do I Do That?

Like set-content, the export-csv cmdlet takes a filename into which it writes a sequence of lines—one per object—with each field separated by a comma:

```
MSH D:\MshScripts> get-process | export-csv -NoTypeInformation processes.csv
```

The resulting file can now be used in an application such as Microsoft Excel or in other tools that can process CSV files. Figure 5-1 shows a graphical representation of handle count by process. The -NoTypeInformation option is used to suppress the first line of the output (which would otherwise contain MSH-specific formatting information).

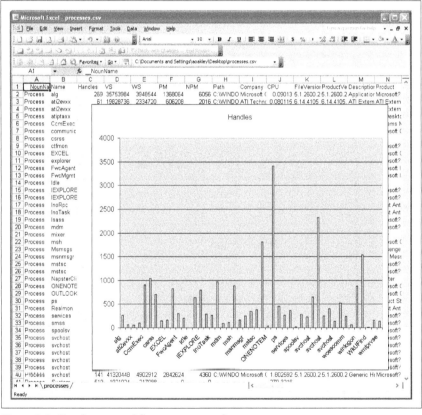

Figure 5-1. Graph generated from get-process data

export-csv also has a mirror cmdlet, import-csv, that takes a CSV file from disk, parses the fields, and generates objects corresponding to each row in the file. Imagine using a spreadsheet to manage a list of batch copy tasks—sources and destinations—used as part of a nightly backup job. A file like the one shown in Example 5-2 could be generated by a program such as Excel.

Example 5-2. BackupTasks.csv

```
Name,Source,Destination
"Copy logs from PRIMARYWEB",\\primaryweb\logs,\\bigdisk\logs\primaryweb
"Copy logs from SECONDWEB",\\secondweb\logs,\\bigdisk\logs\secondweb
"Backup user dirs on FS",\\fs\users,\\bigdisk\userdirs
"Backup INTRA wwwroot",\\intra\wwwroot,\\bigdisk\intra
```

Using import-csv and foreach, it's possible to work through the list of tasks systematically, performing each in turn:

```
MSH D:\MshScripts> $tasks = import-csv BackupTasks.csv
MSH D:\MshScripts> foreach ($task in $tasks) {
>>echo $task.Name
>>robocopy /s $task.Source $task.Destination
>>}
>>
Copy logs from PRIMARYWEB

-------------------------------------------------------------------------------
   ROBOCOPY     ::     Robust File Copy for Windows     ::     Version XP010
-------------------------------------------------------------------------------

  Started : Tue May 31 18:48:10 2005

   Source : \\primaryweb\logs
     Dest : \\bigdisk\logs\primaryweb

    Files : *.*

  Options : *.* /COPY:DAT /R:1000000 /W:30 /S

-------------------------------------------------------------------------------
  ...
```

What About...

...Support for other data formats? MSH can parse XML files to form a structured object that can be used in the pipeline. For nested data, XML is often more convenient than comma-separated formats. Let's take the backup job example a step further, this time creating file lists for each job. The listing in Example 5-3 is an XML representation of two new backup jobs, each defining its own source, destination, and file list.

Example 5-3. BackupTasks.xml

```
<Jobs>
    <Job Name="Backup a and b">
        <Source>\\server1\files</Source>
        <Destination>\\server2\backup</Destination>
        <File>a.txt</File>
        <File>b.txt</File>
    </Job>
    <Job Name="Backup c, d and e">
        <Source>\\server1\files</Source>
        <Destination>\\server3\backup</Destination>
        <File>c.txt</File>
        <File>d.txt</File>
        <File>e.txt</File>
    </Job>
</Jobs>
```

We load the XML file with get-content, *casting* it to an xml type. (We'll see more about casting in the next section.) The resulting $xml variable contains the data, organized in the same fashion as the source file:

```
MSH D:\MshScripts> $xml = [Xml]$(get-content BackupTasks.xml)
MSH D:\MshScripts> $xml

Jobs
----
Jobs
```

It's now possible to use standard MSH language to work through the jobs in order, iterating through the collections that are defined in the XML file:

```
MSH D:\MshScripts> foreach ($job in $xml.Jobs.Job) {
>>$job.Name
>>foreach ($file in $job.File) {
>>   $source = combine-path $job.Source $file
>>   $dest = combine-path $job.Destination $file
>>   copy-item $source $dest
>>}
>>}
>>
Backup a and b
Backup c, d and e
```

Each deeper level of the XML file can be accessed from within the shell using dot notation. $xml.Jobs.Job gives the collection of <*Job*> elements for that job, $job.File gives the collection of <File> elements for that job, and so on.

Where Can I Learn More?

import-csv and export-csv both have additional usage information available through get-help. We'll see more of the .NET Framework Class Library (which provides the support for XML documents) in the next section and in the upcoming section, "Calling Methods of the .NET Class Library."

How Variables Relate to the .NET Framework

Scattered across the examples we've seen so far have been a number of references to the .NET Framework, which was introduced in Chapter 3. We'll now take some time to look at the deep relationship between MSH and the .NET Framework and several of the ways that it brings additional functionality to the shell.

Given the number of classes available in the Class Library, it's impossible to cover each in turn. We'll look at a few examples that lead the way and illustrate what the tight integration with the .NET Framework allows. An understanding of what is possible will likely become invaluable as you use MSH to approach more tasks that are increasingly complex.

How Do I Do That?

Let's start by reviewing a syntax we've already encountered: square brackets ([ ]). When square brackets are used in a script, they indicate to the shell that the enclosed term is a .NET Framework reference. A reference may be in the form of a *fully qualified class* (such as [System.Xml.XmlDocument]), a class name within the System namespace (such as [string]), or one of several shortcuts (such as [Xml] and [Regex]).

We've already encountered different variable types (such as int, double, string), and it is no coincidence that each one is based on a .NET class. MSH does its best to automatically infer underlying types when working with data. The type conversion rules follow a predictable pattern. If the value looks like a number, it will be converted to either an int (whole number) or a double (real number), depending on whether a decimal point is present. Anything else must be enclosed in quotation marks and is assumed to be a string:

```
MSH D:\MshScripts> $a = 132
# $a is an int

MSH D:\MshScripts> $b = 3.14
# $b is a double
```

```
MSH D:\MshScripts> $c = 0x20
# $c is an int with value 32 (decimal)

MSH D:\MshScripts> $d = "99.99"
# $d is a string
```

Automatic type conversion also happens when operations are performed on variables. In the case of addition, using + on a double and an int will yield a double: in general, MSH will try to preserve as much precision as possible during arithmetic operations:

```
MSH D:\MshScripts> $a = 1.2
MSH D:\MshScripts> $b = 3
MSH D:\MshScripts> $c = $a + $b
# $c is a double with value 4.2
```

At times it's necessary to override these rules by using an *explicit cast*. Using the square bracket notation before either the variable name or the value, a script can force MSH to convert a value to a suitable type for either the immediate assignment or all future ones:

```
MSH D:\MshScripts> $a = [int]3.21
MSH D:\MshScripts> $a                    # round 3.21 to an int this time only 3
MSH D:\MshScripts> $a = 5.2
MSH D:\MshScripts> $a
5.2
MSH D:\MshScripts> [int]$b = 1.2      # any future assignments to $b will be
                                         rounded
MSH D:\MshScripts> $b
1
MSH D:\MshScripts> $b = 6.9           # since $b is always an int, round up to 7
MSH D:\MshScripts> $b
7
MSH D:\MshScripts> $a = "samplestring"
MSH D:\MshScripts> $b = "samplestring"
: Cannot convert "samplestring" to "System.Int32". Error: "samplestring is
not a valid value for Int32.".
At line:1 char:3
+ $b= <<<< "samplestring"
```

Casting can be used to convert values into any .NET Framework type, not just into the native int, double, and string cases we've seen so far. For example, the boolean type represents a true/false value, and explicit cast to this type will convert a value into one of those states. Many other types can parse a string into a format they are well suited to represent:

```
MSH D:\MshScripts> $success = [boolean]1
MSH D:\MshScripts> $success
True
```

```
MSH D:\MshScripts> $success = [boolean]0
False

MSH D:\MshScripts> $moonDay = [datetime]"1969-5-20"
MSH D:\MshScripts> $moonDay

Tuesday, May 20, 1969 12:00:00 AM

MSH D:\MshScripts> $newYear = [datetime]"1/1"
MSH D:\MshScripts> $newYear

Saturday, January 01, 2005 12:00:00 AM
```

We've covered some of this ground before, but this recap sets the scene for what comes next. A new concept that we haven't covered yet is *enumeration*, which defines a (usually small) set of valid values. A variable is assigned an enumeration value using an explicit cast of a string. Some enumerations allow multiple values (known as *flags*), which can be specified as a comma-separated list:

```
MSH D:\MshScripts> $succ = [System.Security.AccessControl.
AuditFlags]"Success"
MSH D:\MshScripts> $both = [System.Security.AccessControl.
AuditFlags]"Success,Failure"
```

All possible values for a given enumeration can be gathered by using the GetNames static method of the Enum class:

```
MSH D:\MshScripts> [Enum]::GetNames([System.Security.AccessControl.
AuditFlags])
None
Success
Failure
```

Flags and enumerations are frequently used when calling into .NET Framework methods, as we'll see in the next section.

What Just Happened?

When variables were first covered in Chapter 3, we quickly saw that they store not only values but also some information about their structure. Instead of treating everything as if it were a string, this distinction is what sets MSH apart from *cmd.exe* and other shells. What we've seen here isn't just a mapping between MSH variable types and .NET Framework types; they are one and the same. A .NET Framework type can be used seamlessly anywhere within the shell.

Although automatic type conversion is designed to go unnoticed, it is helpful to understand the predictable pattern used by the shell when figuring out the type for a variable. For assignment, the shell follows this sequence:

- If the variable does not have a strict type:
  - If the value is a number without a decimal point (of the form 123 or 0x123, 12e3, 16k, or similar), the variable is an `int`.
  - If the value is a number with a decimal point (of the form 123.45, 123.0, 12.3e4, or similar), the variable is a `double`.
  - If the value is contained within quotation marks (single or double), the variable is a `string`.
  - If none of the above applies, the value is evaluated as a cmdlet, function, or executable program, and its type will vary depending on what is invoked.
- If the variable already has a type (it was created with explicit type before the variable name):
  - Try to convert the value to the variable's type. If an automatic conversion fails, an error will be displayed.

Automatic type conversion stops short of trying to make too many assumptions because sometimes there is too little information in the assignment or operation for MSH to accurately judge what it should be doing. Explicit casts are used to fill this gap and provide the means for telling the shell exactly which types to use. Some degree of caution is a good idea when casting between different types. While MSH will put a stop to nonsensical operations (`[bool]($b*"s")`), other conversions are legitimate (`[int]$b` where $b is a boolean) but may not always have the desired or expected effect. Although it is sometimes possible to just "make it work" by casting one type to another, it's generally a good idea to understand why it wasn't working in the first place.

Where Can I Learn More?

Refer to Chapter 3, where we first discussed variables. The types available in the System namespace are listed on MSDN: *http://msdn.microsoft.com/library/default.asp?url=/library/en-us/cpref/html/frlrfsystem.asp*.

That's only half the story. Now that you understand that MSH types and .NET Framework types are one and the same, let's look at using this rich set of methods in the Class Library.

Calling Methods of the .NET Class Library

Although it may not have been readily apparent, MSH has been heavily utilizing the .NET Framework in many of the examples we've seen so far. While an expression like (get-process).Count gives the number we're expecting, the Count part is actually referring to a property that all array classes have: their size.

The dot notation is used to indicate to the shell that we're interested in a specific property of an object. This is the means by which $dt.Day can give the day part of a date. Properties of properties can be expressed by appending another period and property name, as in (get-process msh).Modules. Count, where Modules is a property of Process, and Count is a property of Modules. This sequencing of a property of a property of a property can go to an arbitrary depth, limited only by the complexity of the objects being processed.

Properties aren't the only use for this versatile dot symbol. Because .NET classes typically offer a set of methods that allow some action related to the object they represent, we can also use this notation for invoking methods.

How Do I Do That?

By now, the string class should be familiar, so we'll start there. Strings have a set of methods for string manipulation, including extraction of partial substrings, matching of phrases, and search and replace. Like accessing a property, methods are called by using a dot between the variable name and the method name. A method invocation also requires a pair of parentheses after the method name, which may contain zero or more parameters separated by commas. Some methods are *overloaded*, meaning that they may behave slightly differently based on their parameters:

```
MSH D:\MshScripts> $a = "Hello, World!"
MSH D:\MshScripts> $a.Substring(7)
World!
MSH D:\MshScripts> $a.Substring(0, 5)
Hello
MSH D:\MshScripts> $a.StartsWith("He")
True
MSH D:\MshScripts> $b = $a.Replace("World", "everyone")
MSH D:\MshScripts> $b
Hello, everyone!
```

Some classes also expose what are known as *static methods* and *static properties*. Instead of operating on a particular object, they can be called or used from the class directly. In these cases, a double colon (::) is used between the class name and its static method or property:

```
MSH D:\MshScripts> $currentTime = [System.DateTime]::Now
# equivalent to get-date

MSH D:\MshScripts> [System.Diagnostics.Process]::Start("calc.exe")
# just "calc.exe" is easier, but this illustrates the point
```

Finally, there's one more cmdlet to meet: new-object. For .NET types, new-object creates an object when given a class name. If additional parameters are supplied, they are used to identify a class constructor with matching parameters.

```
MSH D:\MshScripts> $myVersion = new-object System.Version 1,2,3,4
MSH D:\MshScripts> $myVersion

Major  Minor  Build  Revision
-----  -----  -----  --------
1      2      3      4
```

What Just Happened?

If this is your first encounter with object-oriented programming and the .NET Framework, don't give up hope. Methods are very similar to MSH functions in that they take a set of parameters and usually return a value after doing some work. Remember, we've been working with objects all along and cmdlets, like get-member, remain useful when exploring the Class Library.

Classes in the Class Library usually include a set of methods that are useful for working on the data they represent. For example, we saw how the String class contains methods for the extract part of a string, whereas the DateTime class provides methods for working with dates, such as adding days and months (while respecting month and year boundaries). The method names themselves describe, in a general sense, what effect they have. For example, the Substring operation of the String class does imply that we'll get back only part of the string. However, there are a number of ways this could be achieved, and this is where method overloading comes in. An overloaded method will do one of a related set of operations, depending on the parameters it is given. Whether we want all of a string after a certain point, just a middle fragment, or just the start of it, we use Substring to get it. get-member can be used to show the different overloads for a given method:

```
MSH D:\MshScripts> [string]"" | get-member –MemberType Method | where-object
{ $_.Name –eq "substring" } | format-list

TypeName   : System.String
Name       : Substring
MemberType : Method
Definition : System.String Substring(Int32 startIndex), System.String
             Substring
             (Int32 startIndex, Int32 length)
```

For each class in the Class Library, there is documentation on MSDN that describes the methods and their behavior in detail and lists any overloaded methods. Static methods and properties generally apply to a whole family of objects rather than to a specific instance. Think of the `DateTime` class, for instance. While methods like `AddDays` and `AddMonths` would act on a particular date, the current date, for example, is a more general idea across all `DateTime` classes. To use static methods and properties, it is not necessary to have a real object in hand (so there will be no `$obj` type of variable); instead, the `::` syntax is used. Its use is similar to the dot notation (the `::` is placed after the class name and before the method or property), but it explicitly tells the shell whether we're interested in using a static property or method.

`new-object` is very similar to the `[ ]` notation. `new-object` is convenient for use in a script where the class constructor performs some useful configuration or setup of the object it creates. In the `System.Version` case, the constructor takes four parameters representing major, minor, build, and revision numbers, respectively. Instead of having to do `$myVersion.Major = 1`; `$myVersion.Minor = 2`; and so on, use the `new-object` syntax, which is usually more compact.

What About…

…Using the `new-object` technique to write shell extensions? Although the `new-object` allows .NET types to be used and manipulated by the shell, it's not always the best approach for building an extension. If you have some existing business logic library that would be valuable from within the shell without changes, then `new-object` style could be very effective.

Where Can I Learn More?

The .NET Class Library documentation is available at *http://msdn.microsoft.com* and gives a list of properties and methods available for every class in the library. All of the public methods listed in the output of `get-member` have accompanying documentation on this site.

As expected, the `get-help` output for `new-object` also lists the options available when creating objects with the cmdlet.

Using new-object with COM Objects

There is one option on the `new-object` cmdlet that deserves further attention. Although most of the examples so far have focused on objects, classes, and all things related to the .NET Framework, the `-ComObject` option opens up a whole new world of possibilities via the Component Object Model (more commonly known as COM).

new-object allows COM objects, which include ActiveX controls, to be used just like any other kind of object within MSH. Because many applications expose an object model for programmability, it is possible to use the familiar MSH cmdlets to interact with many different tools and applications that already exist on a machine.

How Do I Do That?

Using new-object to instantiate a COM object is very similar to the process used for .NET classes, and it just requires the addition of the -ComObject option:

```
MSH D:\MshScripts> $ie = new-object -ComObject "InternetExplorer.
Application"
```

There is nothing particularly special about the $ie variable aside from the fact that it's representing a type that we haven't used yet. get-member will quickly help us find out more information about the object model exposed by Internet Explorer:

```
MSH D:\MshScripts> $ie | get-member -MemberType Method


    TypeName: System.__ComObject#{d30c1661-cdaf-11d0-8a3e-00c04fc9e26e}

Name                MemberType Definition
----                ---------- ----------
ClientToWindow      Method     void ClientToWindow (int, int)
ExecWB              Method     void ExecWB (OLECMDID, OLECMDEXECOPT, Variant,
                               Var...
GetProperty         Method     Variant GetProperty (string)
GoBack              Method     void GoBack ()
GoForward           Method     void GoForward ()
GoHome              Method     void GoHome ()
GoSearch            Method     void GoSearch ()
Navigate            Method     void Navigate (string, Variant, Variant, Variant,
                               ...
Navigate2           Method     void Navigate2 (Variant, Variant, Variant,
                               Variant...
PutProperty         Method     void PutProperty (string, Variant)
QueryStatusWB       Method     OLECMDF QueryStatusWB (OLECMDID)
Quit                Method     void Quit ()
Refresh             Method     void Refresh ()
Refresh2            Method     void Refresh2 (Variant)
ShowBrowserBar      Method     void ShowBrowserBar (Variant, Variant, Variant)
Stop                Method     void Stop ()
```

Let's try one of the overloaded Navigate methods, which takes a single URL as the target. We'll also set the Visible property to true so that we can actually see what is going on:

```
MSH D:\MshScripts> $ie.Navigate("http://www.oreilly.com")
MSH D:\MshScripts> $ie.Visible = $true
```

At this point, an Internet Explorer window, already navigating its way over the Web toward the O'Reilly web site, should become visible.

The Windows graphical shell (EXPLORER) also exposes several methods through a Shell.Application COM interface. We can use this interface to call up the folder browser:

```
MSH D:\MshScripts> $ui = new-object -ComObject "Shell.Application"
MSH D:\MshScripts> $path = $ui.BrowseForFolder(0, "Select a folder", 0, 0)
```

At this point, the folder-selection dialog box (like the one shown in Figure 5-2) will appear and the script will wait until the dialog is dismissed.

Figure 5-2. Browse For Folder dialog box

If OK was selected, the $path variable will contain information relating to the selection. The full path of the selected folder can be found in the $path. Self.Path property.

What's Next?

After having read this chapter, it is fair to say that we've seen a good cross-section of the functionality within MSH. Of course, there is plenty more to discover and experimentation is the best way to learn. In the final two chapters, we'll start looking at some task-focused problems and see how MSH can make day-to-day administrative tasks much easier.

## CHAPTER 6

Working with Operating System Components

As an administration tool, MSH offers a range of cmdlets that give script authors and administrators access to most of the major stores of data within the operating system. In this chapter, we'll take a look at the data sources that are readily available in MSH, from event logs to WMI, and the cmdlets that are available for making changes to operating system components.

Monitoring the Event Log

The operating system provides the event log service as a mechanism for allowing the system and applications running on it to record their activity in a nonintrusive fashion. If each operating system component and application decided to pop up a message whenever anything happened, an interactive user would never have a chance to get anything done. While the Event Viewer tool (*eventvwr.exe*) continues to allow an administrator to review, sort, and filter events from a graphical interface, MSH also provides a cmdlet for querying the event logs from within the shell.

Windows operating systems primarily store event records in three logs, separating events based on their relevance to different aspects of the system.

Application log
> The application log is the place in which applications running on the system can record events of note. It's up to the application developer to determine which events are recorded in this log.

Security log
> The security log records activity related to user and system authorization and authentication: failed login attempts, file creation, deletion, and modification are captured here.

System log
> Operating system components use the system log to record their activity. If a driver fails to initialize some hardware, a service fails to start, or the machine itself reboots, an entry will be placed in this log.

The event log framework is extensible, meaning that installed applications and optional operating system components (such as the DNS Service) can create their own logs into which they record their events. In fact, MSH creates a MonadLog event log used for storing startup, shutdown, and other critical events related to the shell.

Let's look at some alternative ways of accessing event log records through MSH.

How Do I Do That?

First, let's introduce the get-eventlog cmdlet, which exposes the event log data to the shell:

```
MSH D:\MshScripts> get-eventlog -list

Max(K) Retain OverflowAction        Entries Name
------ ------ --------------        ------- ----
15,232      0 OverwriteAsNeeded         231 Application
15,360      0 OverwriteAsNeeded         305 MonadLog
30,016      0 OverwriteAsNeeded       5,407 Security
15,168      0 OverwriteAsNeeded         371 System
```

On a typical system, we see these four logs and some information about their size and what happens when the log reaches capacity (its overwrite behavior). Let's focus on the security log for a moment. get-eventlog can be called with the -newest option, which can be used to limit the number of records to return. Because event logs can potentially contain many thousands of entries, it's convenient and efficient to limit the number of records returned:

```
MSH D:\MshScripts> get-eventlog Security -newest 10

Index Time        Type Source        EventID Message
----- ----        ---- ------        ------- -------
 5407 Aug 22 23:05 Succ Security          520 The system time was c...
 5406 Aug 22 23:05 Succ Security          520 The system time was c...
 5405 Aug 22 23:05 Succ Security          520 The system time was c...
 5404 Aug 22 23:05 Succ Security          520 The system time was c...
 5403 Aug 22 23:05 Succ Security          520 The system time was c...
 5402 Aug 22 23:05 Succ Security          520 The system time was c...
 5401 Aug 22 23:05 Succ Security          520 The system time was c...
 5400 Aug 22 23:05 Succ Security          520 The system time was c...
 5399 Aug 22 23:05 Succ Security          520 The system time was c...
 5398 Aug 22 23:05 Succ Security          520 The system time was c...
```

Of course, the list of events here is actually a sequence of objects that have been placed into the pipeline. The familiar where-object and format-table cmdlets work well on pipeline objects, so we can start filtering and tabulating results right away. In this example, we'll look for only those events that represent a successful login and tabulate the time and username associated with the event:

```
MSH D:\MshScripts> get-eventlog Security -newest 1000 | where-object { $_.
EventID -eq 528 } | format-table TimeGenerated,Username

TimeGenerated                         UserName
-------------                         --------
8/22/2005 8:42:47 PM                  MONAD\andy
8/22/2005 8:22:08 PM                  MONAD\andy
8/22/2005 6:42:07 PM                  MONAD\andy
8/22/2005 5:59:25 PM                  MONAD\andy
8/22/2005 4:50:20 PM                  MONAD\andy
8/22/2005 1:42:30 PM                  MONAD\andy
...
```

There is no reason to filter only by event IDs. Let's say we're just focused on looking at system errors: we might instead choose to filter just those records with their EntryType property set to the Error. Other values that could be used include FailureAudit, Information, SuccessAudit, and Warning. Note that even though we tell get-eventlog to return 1,000 records at most, we might see significantly fewer because, of those 1,000, many may be informational or warning events:

```
MSH D:\MshScripts> get-eventlog System -newest 1000 | where-object { $_.
EntryType -eq "Error"}

Index Time          Type Source       EventID Message
----- ----          ---- ------       ------- -------
  520 Aug 24 20:05  Erro DCOM           10016 The application-speci...
  518 Aug 24 20:05  Erro W32Time     39452701 The time provider Ntp...
  515 Aug 24 20:05  Erro NETLOGON        5719 This computer was not...
  508 Aug 24 20:05  Erro EventLog        6008 The previous system s...
  505 Aug 23 09:05  Erro Tcpip           4199 The system detected a...
  502 Aug 23 09:05  Erro Tcpip           4199 The system detected a...
  501 Aug 23 08:05  Erro Tcpip           4199 The system detected a...
...
```

Because the event log is time-based, we'll often prefer to filter events on the same date range or a sliding window. The where-object cmdlet can be used to filter just those event log entries within a given range by performing tests on the TimeGenerated property:

```
MSH D:\MshScripts> get-eventlog System | where-object { ($_.TimeGenerated
-gt "2005-8-22") -and ($_.TimeGenerated -lt "2005-8-23") }
```

```
Index Time            Type Source            EventID Message
----- ----            ---- ------            ------- -------
  369 Aug 22 20:05    Warn DnsApi             11197 The system failed to
                                                    ...
  368 Aug 22 20:05    Info Service Control M...  7036 The WinHTTP Web
                                                    Proxy...
  367 Aug 22 20:05    Info WinHttpAutoProxySvc  12517 The WinHTTP Web
                                                    Proxy...
  364 Aug 22 20:05    Info Service Control M...  7035 The WinHTTP Web
                                                    Proxy...
  363 Aug 22 19:05    Warn DnsApi             11197 The system failed to
                                                    ...
  362 Aug 22 18:05    Warn DnsApi             11197 The system failed to
                                                    ...
  361 Aug 22 17:05    Erro NETLOGON            5719 This computer was
                                                    not...
  360 Aug 22 17:05    Warn DnsApi             11197 The system failed to
                                                    ...
  359 Aug 22 16:05    Warn DnsApi             11197 The system failed to
                                                    ...
  358 Aug 22 15:05    Warn DnsApi             11197 The system failed to
                                                    ...
...
```

It's also possible to use a dynamic date range by using the methods of the DateTime class. Let's say we want to look at the last 24 hours: we can use the AddHours method to get the exact date and time of 24 hours ago and use that in the where-object test:

```
MSH D:\MshScripts> get-eventlog System | where-object { $_.TimeGenerated -gt
(get-date).AddHours(-24) }

Index Time            Type Source            EventID Message
----- ----            ---- ------            ------- -------
  538 Aug 24 20:05    Warn W32Time          39452686 The time provider
                                                    Ntp...
  537 Aug 24 20:05    Info Service Control M...  7036 The Windows
                                                    Installer...
  536 Aug 24 20:05    Info Windows Update Agent    22 Restart Required: To
                                                    ...
  535 Aug 24 20:05    Info Windows Update Agent    19 Installation
                                                    Successf...
  534 Aug 24 20:05    Info NtServicePack       921881 Windows Server 2003
                                                    H...
  533 Aug 24 20:05    Info Windows Update Agent    19 Installation
                                                    Successf...
  532 Aug 24 20:05    Info Service Control M...  7035 The SMS Process
                                                    Event...
  531 Aug 24 20:05    Info Windows Update Agent    18 Installation Ready:
                                                    T...
...
```

What Just Happened?

All of the read access to the event log is provided through a single cmdlet. Depending on its command-line options, it can be used to list available logs or to reveal their contents. As we've seen before, the get-member cmdlet can be used to discover the available fields of the EventLogEntry objects that get-eventlog generates. We looked at some of the interesting fields for sorting and filtering—EventID, EventType, and TimeGenerated—but others, including Source, Message, Category, and Index, also contain valuable information.

Filtering by date ranges can be especially useful when writing scripts that call out to external programs that might write their diagnostic information to the event log. By recording the time at the start of a script, it's possible to then report on any new event log entries that were created during the run. Example 6-1 shows a pseudoscript that could be used to save events to a file.

Example 6-1. List events generated during a script run

```
$startTime = (get-date)

# do some work
# call out to external tools

get-eventlog Application | where-object { $_.TimeGenerated -gt $startTime } |
format-list | out-file ScriptGeneratedEventLog.txt
```

What About...

...Using this cmdlet for monitoring system health? Certainly. A script built around get-eventlog could be run periodically as a Scheduled Task. When run, it could look at all events logged since the last run and take action if any indicated a problem. While this approach works well for small systems, it may not be as easy to manage in larger deployments where tools such as Microsoft Operations Manager are better suited to the task.

The .NET Framework holds a range of methods that allow even more interaction with the event log system. Calling into the System.Diagnostics. EventLog class, it's simple to create a new event record and add it to the Application log:

```
MSH D:\MshScripts> [System.Diagnostics.EventLog]::WriteEntry("ProcessFiles.
msh", "Completed successfully")
```

Furthermore, an administrator can create and remove new event logs by using other methods within the same class. For example, we can use the following to create and remove a new event log called PrivateLog. After creation, this new event log will appear in the output of get-eventlog -list, as well as in the graphical *eventvwr.exe* tool. This could be useful as part of a deployment script for a large application in which specialized logging is required; in typical script and administration, it's more common to log notices to the Application log:

```
# create a new empty log called PrivateLog
MSH D:\MshScripts> [System.Diagnostics.EventLog]::
CreateEventSource("ProcessFiles.msh", "PrivateLog")
# delete log and all entries
MSH D:\MshScripts> [System.Diagnostics.EventLog]::Delete("PrivateLog")
```

Where Can I Learn More?

Help for the get-eventlog cmdlet has a review of the functionality we've covered here, with additional details on other command-line options. The MSDN documentation for the EventLog class contains details about some of the more advanced tasks: *http://msdn.microsoft.com/library/default.asp?url=/ library/en-us/cpref/html/frlrfSystemDiagnosticsEventLogClassTopic.asp*. Also, the event ID lookup tool (*http://www.eventid.net*) is a useful resource when working with event logs.

Now, let's focus our attention on another part of the system plumbing: NT services.

If you've tried to use *sc.exe* from within MSH, you may have noticed that the experience isn't quite what you'd expect. Instead of communicating with the Service Controller, you may be presented with an obscure prompt complaining about missing parameters.

On startup, MSH creates an alias sc that points to set-content. This alias actually masks the underlying tool (since MSH always tries to run any aliases first), so typing SC from a prompt won't run the underlying program. To work around this behavior, use both the tool name and extension: SC.EXE.

Auditing System Services

Many of the subsystems running on a Windows machine run as background processes, known as services, that have no direct interaction with a user's session. The components that exist as services are varied and include everything from the application-level Internet Information Services (IIS) and DNS Server to system plumbing of the Remote Procedure Call (RPC) and logon infrastructure. Services can be configured, started, and stopped from within the Services Administrative Tool, and command-line control of system services is available through the net start and net stop commands, as well as the *sc.exe* tool. MSH offers several cmdlets that complement the existing management tools and allow scripts to discover, interrogate, and manage the state of services within the shell in a consistent fashion.

How Do I Do That?

Let's start by getting a picture of the different services registered with the system. The get-service cmdlet, when called with no options, generates a list of all registered services, including their present state:

```
MSH D:\MshScripts> get-service

Status   Name             DisplayName
------   ----             -----------
Stopped  Alerter          Alerter
Stopped  ALG              Application Layer Gateway Service
Stopped  AppMgmt          Application Management
Stopped  aspnet_state     ASP.NET State Service
Running  AudioSrv         Windows Audio
Stopped  BITS             Background Intelligent Transfer Ser...
Stopped  Browser          Computer Browser
Running  CcmExec          SMS Agent Host
Stopped  CiSvc            Indexing Service
Stopped  ClipSrv          ClipBook
Stopped  COMSysApp        COM+ System Application
Running  CryptSvc         Cryptographic Services
Running  DcomLaunch       DCOM Server Process Launcher
Stopped  Dfs              Distributed File System
Running  Dhcp             DHCP Client
Stopped  dmadmin          Logical Disk Manager Administrative...
Running  dmserver         Logical Disk Manager
Running  Dnscache         DNS Client
...
```

Given the long list of services registered (note that not all are running), it's convenient to use where-object to reduce the list to active services only. get-service will optionally take a service name, which can include wildcard characters:

```
MSH D:\MshScripts> get-service | where-object { $_.Status -eq "Running" }

Status   Name             DisplayName
------   ----             -----------
Running  AudioSrv         Windows Audio
Running  CcmExec          SMS Agent Host
Running  CryptSvc         Cryptographic Services
Running  DcomLaunch       DCOM Server Process Launcher
```

```
Running  Dhcp              DHCP Client
Running  dmserver          Logical Disk Manager
Running  Dnscache          DNS Client
Running  ERSvc             Error Reporting Service
Running  Eventlog          Event Log
Running  EventSystem       COM+ Event System
Running  helpsvc           Help and Support
...

MSH D:\MshScripts> get-service t*

Status   Name              DisplayName
------   ----              -----------
Stopped  TapiSrv           Telephony
Running  TermService       Terminal Services
Stopped  Themes            Themes
Stopped  TlntSvr           Telnet
Stopped  TrkSvr            Distributed Link Tracking Server
Running  TrkWks            Distributed Link Tracking Client
Stopped  Tssdis            Terminal Services Session Directory
```

Let's take a look at the Telnet service (TlntSvr) to see what additional information we can extract from get-service:

```
MSH D:\MshScripts> $telnet=get-service tlntsvr
MSH D:\MshScripts> $telnet | format-list


Name               : TlntSvr
DisplayName        : Telnet
Status             : Stopped
DependentServices  : {}
ServicesDependedOn : {RPCSS, NTLMSSP, TCPIP}
CanPauseAndContinue : False
CanShutdown        : False
CanStop            : False
ServiceType        : Win32OwnProcess
```

On this machine, we can see that the service, as well as some information about related services, is currently stopped. Because the ServicesDependedOn property is actually a list of other related services, let's have MSH show the running status of each of the services that Telnet needs in order to start:

```
MSH D:\MshScripts> foreach ($dependency in $telnet.ServicesDependedOn) {
>>write-host "$($dependency.Name) is $($dependency.Status)"
>>}
>>
RPCSS is Running
NTLMSSP is Stopped
TCPIP is Running
```

On this machine, the Telnet service is not just stopped, it's actually disabled. MSH provides the set-service cmdlet for changing service configuration. In this case, we can use the -StartupType option to put the service in a position in which it can be started and use start-service to get it running. The stop-service cmdlet is used to terminate a running service and bring it back to a stopped state:

```
MSH D:\MshScripts> set-service TlntSvr -StartupType Manual
MSH D:\MshScripts> start-service TlntSvr
# telnet service running
MSH D:\MshScripts> stop-service TlntSvr
```

 Service configuration through set-service relates to the very basic startup type, name, and description. Service-specific configuration is not possible through this cmdlet: tasks such as managing web sites in IIS or configuring for Terminal Services are handled elsewhere.

What Just Happened?

The get-service cmdlet generates a series of ServiceController objects and pumps them into the pipeline. Each object contains a set of information about the service it represents, as well as a set of methods for basic service control. The start-service and stop-service cmdlets will try to make changes to the running state of a service but are still subject to the rules of the services system. In other words, trying to start a disabled service will still result in a failure, as will trying to stop a required service.

Although it's tempting to run through the list of services a particular service depends on, starting each in turn, it is unnecessary. When a request to start a service is made, Windows is able to determine which services are needed and will start any stopped ones as appropriate. Both the DependentServices and ServicesDependedOn properties are useful for understanding the relationships between the different services, but it is rarely necessary to start and stop dependent services manually.

set-service gives the script author the ability to update service configuration from within MSH and is a great candidate for inclusion in machine setup or deployment scripts. Exercising caution around services is recommended: starting, stopping, or disabling services without planning can cause applications and functionality to break without warning.

In addition to the service-related cmdlets we saw here, there are also cmdlets for restarting (restart-service), suspending (suspend-service), and registering a service with the service subsystem (new-service).

What About...

...Using get-service to check whether services are running before running a script? Yes; with a short foreach loop at the start of the script, it's easy to check that a list of required services is running before executing the main body. In the pseudoscript in Example 6-2, an array is used to store the list of services to be checked, and the script will exit if any of them are not in a running state.

Example 6-2. Checking for dependent services for running a script

```
$requiredServices = @("w3svc", "iisadmin", "messenger")

foreach ($serviceName in $requiredServices)
{
    $service = get-service $serviceName
    if ($service.Status -ne "Running")
    {
        "$serviceName not running!"
        exit
    }
}

# script is good to continue
```

Where Can I Learn More?

More information on *-service cmdlets is available through get-help. The Services management snap-in (available in Control Panel, Administrative Tools) also contains a help system with an overview and list of standard Windows services.

Get System Information from WMI

Windows Management Instrumentation (WMI) is a technology for storing and working with system-management information. It contains representation of the full enterprise ecosystem, including hardware description, system information, and knowledge of application deployment.

MSH makes WMI information available in the shell by means of the get-wmiobject cmdlet. Data within WMI is stored by class, which is a scheme that groups together similar categories of data. In this section, we'll focus on the Win32 classes, which contain the majority of information about a Windows system.

How Do I Do That?

Let's begin by looking at the output of get-wmiobject for a few of the very general classes, such as the system processor and BIOS:

```
MSH D:\MshScripts> get-wmiobject Win32_Processor
```

```
AddressWidth               : 32
Architecture               : 0
Availability               : 3
Caption                    : x86 Family 6 Model 13 Stepping 6
ConfigManagerErrorCode     :
ConfigManagerUserConfig    :
CpuStatus                  : 1
CreationClassName          : Win32_Processor
CurrentClockSpeed          : 1395
CurrentVoltage             :
DataWidth                  : 32
Description                : x86 Family 6 Model 13 Stepping 6
DeviceID                   : CPU0
ErrorCleared               :
ErrorDescription           :
ExtClock                   : 100
Family                     : 2
InstallDate                :
L2CacheSize                : 0
L2CacheSpeed               :
LastErrorCode              :
Level                      : 6
LoadPercentage             : 0
Manufacturer               : GenuineIntel
MaxClockSpeed              : 1395
Name                       : Intel(R) Pentium(R) M processor 1.60GHz
OtherFamilyDescription     :
PNPDeviceID                :
PowerManagementCapabilities :
PowerManagementSupported   : False
ProcessorId                : 07C0A93B000006D6
ProcessorType              : 3
Revision                   : 3334
Role                       : CPU
SocketDesignation          : X1
Status                     : OK
StatusInfo                 : 3
Stepping                   : 6
SystemCreationClassName    : Win32_ComputerSystem
SystemName                 : MONAD
UniqueId                   :
UpgradeMethod              : 10
Version                    : Model 13, Stepping 6
```

```
VoltageCaps              : 6
__GENUS                  : 2
__CLASS                  : Win32_Processor
__SUPERCLASS             : CIM_Processor
__DYNASTY                : CIM_ManagedSystemElement
__RELPATH                : Win32_Processor.DeviceID="CPU0"
__PROPERTY_COUNT         : 44
__DERIVATION             : {CIM_Processor, CIM_LogicalDevice,
                           CIM_LogicalElement, CIM_ManagedSystemElement}
__SERVER                 : MONAD
__NAMESPACE              : root\cimv2
__PATH                   : \\MONAD\root\cimv2:Win32_Processor.DeviceID
                           ="CPU0"

MSH D:\MshScripts> get-wmiobject Win32_BIOS


SMBIOSBIOSVersion : 080002
Manufacturer      : American Megatrends Inc.
Name              : BIOS Date: 08/14/03 19:41:02  Ver: 08.00.02
SerialNumber      : 2265-1368-5332-4363-8258-5715-43
Version           : A M I  - 8000314
```

Although the list of information that comes back from the cmdlet can be quite long in cases, it's returned in the form of a structured object in the pipeline. As such, the standard formatting cmdlets can be used to simplify the output for reading and reporting:

```
MSH D:\MshScripts> get-wmiobject Win32_Processor | format-list
Name,Description,ProcessorID


Name        : Intel(R) Pentium(R) M processor 1.60GHz
Description : x86 Family 6 Model 13 Stepping 6
ProcessorId : 07C0A93B000006D6
```

Some calls to get-wmiobject will result in several objects being created, one for each device (or component) of the class. For example, physical memory is comprised of a number of distinct memory modules that can easily be tabulated for review:

```
MSH D:\MshScripts> get-wmiobject Win32_PhysicalMemory | format-table
Tag,BankLabel,DeviceLocator,Capacity


Tag                BankLabel     DeviceLocator      Capacity
---                ---------     -------------      --------
Physical Memory 0  BANK0         DIMM1              268435456
Physical Memory 1  BANK1         DIMM2              268435456
Physical Memory 2  BANK1         DIMM2              268435456
Physical Memory 3  BANK1         DIMM2              268435456
```

As an enterprise class system for working with management information, WMI works seamlessly across machine boundaries. The get-wmiobject cmdlet will accept a -ComputerName option, which can be used to query the WMI store of another system in the local network. When combined with a small foreach loop, it becomes possible to audit a series of computers for their WMI information:

```
MSH D:\MshScripts> $machines = @("hermes", "zeus", "apollo")
MSH D:\MshScripts> $(
>>foreach ($machine in $machines)
>>{
>>  get-wmiobject Win32_Processor -ComputerName $machine
>>}
>>) | format-table SystemName,Name
>>
SystemName                      Name
----------                      ----
HERMES                          Intel(R) Pentium(R) M processor 1.60GHz
ZEUS                            Intel(R) Pentium(R) 4 CPU 2.8GHz
ZEUS                            Intel(R) Pentium(R) 4 CPU 2.8GHz
APOLLO                          Intel(R) Pentium(R) 4 CPU 2.8GHz
```

The fact that there are two rows in the table for the ZEUS machine is not a bug—in fact, it's a sign that the script is working correctly. Because the ZEUS machine has two CPUs, the output of get-wmiobject is actually an array of two WMI objects, one for each processor.

From here, it's a small step to include more information and build up a CSV file (with export-csv) that will prepare this data for handling inside a spreadsheet or other reporting system.

What Just Happened?

The get-wmiobject is a great window into the operating system and into a machine's hardware. Although these examples focus on the hardware aspects of a system, WMI contains a far richer set of data. The available class names (such as Win32_BIOS) are predefined by the operating system. get-wmiobject can be called with a -list option to generate a list of all available classes in the current WMI namespace. (The default namespace is a good place to start exploring.)

The default formatter understands many of the classes that come from the WMI cmdlet and, in some cases, displays only a few of the relevant properties. Don't be deceived, though, because there's often much more lurking inside. Take the Win32_OperatingSystem class, for example. By default, MSH shows six fields, including system directory, registered owner, and organization. However, pipe the output to format-list with a wildcard option (get-wmiobject Win32_OperatingSystem | format-list *), and the full set of the object's properties and methods is visible.

In the last case, a foreach loop is used to build up the data from a range of machines. Because a foreach loop itself doesn't actually generate any output, we include it inside the evaluation syntax ($(...)). MSH understands that it must first evaluate the entire foreach loop (therefore querying each machine) and collect the objects generated by the loop before passing them downstream to the format-table cmdlet for output.

What About…

Why do you need get-service when you can query the Win32_Service class? Everything seems to be available in WMI. For the two examples we saw earlier in this chapter, the specialized cmdlets exist to make a specific task easier to perform. The output of get-service (especially when combined with a command-line option) is immediately useful from within the shell and makes working with services a relatively simple task.

From the shell, WMI is generally a read-only data store. Although there is no set-wmiobject cmdlet, it is possible to invoke WMI objects through the .NET Framework with InvokeMethod on the System.Management.ManagementObject class. Note that WMI methods are relatively uncommon and can require a lot of work (and caution) to use correctly.

Where Can I Learn More?

The help page for get-wmiobject contains complete details about this cmdlet. In particular, there is support for WMI namespaces beyond the default *root/cimv2* used here. There are also options to use different credentials when querying other machines for information.

The WMI SDK documentation at *http://msdn.microsoft.com/library/default. asp?url=/library/en-us/wmisdk/wmi/operating_system_classes.asp* has complete details of the class names that can be used in queries.

Manage Filesystem Permissions

Besides containing content layout and data, many filesystems also provide a layer of access control defined by a set of permissions granted to users on a per-file or per-folder basis. Although command-line modification of file permissions is possible with the *cacls.exe* tool, MSH also offers two cmdlets, get-acl and set-acl that give scripts access to these *Access Control Lists* (ACLs).

In this section, we'll look at two approaches to managing file permissions. In the first, we'll see the ease with which MSH can use existing command-line tools. In the second, we'll focus on the MSH-specific cmdlets.

How Do I Do That?

We've already seen how foreach can be used to loop through a number of items generated by a cmdlet, so let's start there:

```
MSH D:\MshScripts> foreach ($file in get-childitem) {
>>cacls.exe $file /E /G andy:F
>>}
>>
processed file: C:\tmp\aclchange.msh
processed file: C:\tmp\brownfox.txt
processed file: C:\tmp\output.csv
processed file: C:\tmp\start.msh
```

This isn't all that different from calling *cacls.exe* with a wildcard (*) parameter, so let's take it a step further. In this case, we'll recursively modify the permissions in a complete folder structure (still possible with the /T flag on *cacls.exe*), except for a few files (with the name "private.txt") that we'll leave untouched:

```
MSH D:\MshScripts> foreach ($file in $(get-childitem -recurse)) {
>>if ($file.FullName -notlike "*private.txt")
>>{
>>    cacls.exe $file.FullName /E /G Everyone:R > null
>>    "Changing permissions on $($file.FullName)"
>>}
>>else
>>{
>>    "Preserving permissions on $($file.FullName)"
>>}
>>}
>>
Changing permissions on C:\web\default.aspx
Changing permissions on C:\web\report.aspx
Changing permissions on C:\web\tutorial\default.aspx
Preserving permissions on C:\web\tutorial\private.txt
Changing permissions on C:\web\faq\default.aspx
```

One other practical use is to assign permissions based on folder name. For example, let's consider a shared folder that has named subfolders for individuals. Assuming that the folder names and NT account names match, we can use *cacls.exe* to grant users permission to control their own folders:

```
MSH D:\MshScripts> foreach ($userdir in get-childitem) {
>>cacls.exe $userdir /E /G $($userdir.Name):F
>>}
>>
```

```
processed folder: C:\shared\asmith
processed folder: C:\shared\bobt
processed folder: C:\shared\jdoe
processed folder: C:\shared\john
```

So far, these scenarios could have been addressed with *cacls.exe*, so let's see what additional capabilities the get-acl and set-acl offer from within MSH. get-acl itself is a simple cmdlet: when given a path, it returns a security descriptor with the permissions and audit characteristics of the target:

```
MSH D:\MshScripts> get-childitem | get-acl | where-object { $_.Owner -like
"*andy" }

Path                      Owner                    Access
----                      -----                    ------
brownfox.txt              MONAD\andy               BUILTIN\
Administrators...
```

It's possible to combine the output of get-acl with set-acl to effect changes to the permissions of an object. We can take the ACL from one file and apply it to a series of others; this can be convenient when updating permissions across a set of files:

```
MSH D:\MshScripts> $acl = get-acl c:\files\knownGoodPermissions.txt
MSH D:\MshScripts> foreach ($file in $(get-childitem c:\files)) { set-acl
$file $acl }
```

Because get-acl is actually returning a .NET Framework object that represents the security information, there are several other tasks that become possible. In this next case, we'll create a function that generates system audit rules and add such a rule to a file to have the operating system track any access:

```
MSH D:\MshScripts> function CreateAuditRule {
>>$identity=[System.Security.Principal.NTAccount]"Everyone"
>>$accessMask=[System.Security.AccessControl.
FileSystemRights]"ReadAndExecute"
>>$inheritFlag=[System.Security.AccessControl.InheritanceFlags]"None"
>>$propFlag=[System.Security.AccessControl.PropagationFlags]"None"
>>$auditFlag=[System.Security.AccessControl.AuditFlags]"Success,Failure"
>>$args[0].AuditRuleFactory($identity, $accessMask, 0, $inheritFlag,
$propFlag, $auditFlag)
>>}
>>
MSH D:\MshScripts> $acl = get-acl brownfox.txt
MSH D:\MshScripts> $rule=CreateAuditRule $acl
MSH D:\MshScripts> $acl.AddAuditRule($rule)
MSH D:\MshScripts> set-acl brownfox.txt $acl
```

As shown in Figure 6-1, the Advanced Security Settings dialog in Windows Explorer now indicates that this new audit rule has been added to the file.

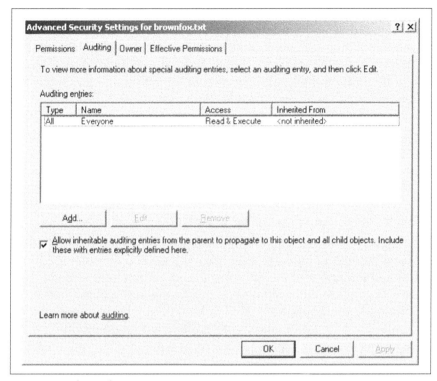

Figure 6-1. Advanced Security Settings

What Just Happened?

We've covered quite a bit of ground here, so let's go back to the beginning and look at the techniques used in each case.

In the first set of examples, MSH was just providing the mechanism for looping through a list of files, while the actual work was being carried out by the existing *cacls.exe* tool. Although the foreach syntax is probably familiar to you by now, the & notation is not. We'll look at this in greater detail in Chapter 7, but, at a simple level, the token just instructs MSH to execute the command that follows it. Because *cacls.exe* fails to match any aliases, functions, or cmdlets, MSH will use the copy of the tool present in the Windows system folder. The structure and format of the options provided to the tool are specific to *cacls.exe*; it's not an MSH cmdlet and, therefore, it isn't subject to the consistent syntax rules offered by the shell.

get-acl can be used in two ways but has a similar function in both. We first saw it included in a pipeline, taking the output of get-childitem and filling the pipeline with data about the access-control lists and audit rules. Generic cmdlets, such as where-object, can then be used to further process access-control information. Remember, get-member can be used to find out more information about the objects generated by get-acl than just the owner name.

The second get-acl form takes a path as an option. In this case, several ACL objects might be generated if the path contains any wildcards. Because these objects represent security and audit rules only, they are portable and can be reapplied to other items in the filesystem without any side effects to the actual content. It's not necessary to look at or modify the object in these cases—it can be passed right through to set-acl.

When modifying or changing security permissions or audit rules, the process does become a little more complicated. The set-acl cmdlet is a lightweight tool for applying a set of permissions to an object. If we don't have immediate access to those permissions or rules (by, say, copying them from another object with get-acl), we need to use the .NET Framework classes to make changes. That's where the CreateAuditRule function comes in.

Although the CreateAuditRule function appears complex, it serves a simple task: it uses a method to create a new audit rule. The first five lines of the function are responsible for setting up the options used to create a new rule. They include the users that the rule applies to; the type of access to track; whether to include rules from parent containers; whether to push this rule onto contents of a folder; and, lastly, whether to track successes, failures, or both. Each of these options is cast as a .NET Framework type, as required by the AuditRuleFactory method. The function eventually calls the method and returns the resulting audit rule.

With the new audit rule in hand, we can add it to the security object given back to us from get-acl using the AddAuditRule method. At this stage, $acl contains both the original information and the extra rule, but as yet no changes have been made to the filesystem. The last step uses set-acl to update the filesystem with the new rule.

What About...

We only scratched the surface of the information that is returned by get-acl. There's a lot of information available in the returned ACL object that can be used in different cases. For example, the $acl.Access property contains a collection of permissions associated with a file, blending both explicit and inherited permissions.

With the cmdlets we've already covered, it is also possible to manage security permissions in a spreadsheet and have an MSH script that updates the real filesystem to reflect any changes. Imagine a spreadsheet that contains file and folder information row by row, with a separate column for usernames that have certain types of access. Using import-csv, a script could loop through each record and make any permission changes using the set-acl cmdlet or *cacls.exe* tool.

Where Can I Learn More?

The *cacls.exe* tool provides some usage information when called with a /? option from the command line. More usage information for the get-acl and set-acl cmdlets is available through get-help.

What's Next?

With a broad base of different MSH techniques in place, we can now look at solving some practical problems. The next chapter will focus on real-world tasks and cover some strategies for turning existing batch files and scripts into MSH scripts.

## CHAPTER 7

Putting MSH to Work

In this book, we've covered a number of MSH's new features and explored some areas that separate it from other shells available today. Some of these changes are significant and some are subtle, but it's clear that the command shell is different with MSH. In this final chapter, we'll look at some applied uses of MSH, including more advanced script techniques, and wrap up with a series of small, task-focused examples.

Invoke Commands with &

If you've been exploring the shell, you may have noticed that MSH and *cmd.exe* treat filenames differently. For example, if a file is dragged from Explorer onto the command prompt window in MSH, the window still acts as though the filename were typed in, but the behavior can differ.

For example, dragging a file *HelloWorld.exe* from the folder *D:\Apps* in an Explorer window onto either a *cmd.exe* or MSH window will result in "D:\ Apps\HelloWorld.exe" being typed at the prompt. However, Examples 7-1 and 7-2 show how the two shells differ in their interpretation of the action.

Example 7-1. Entering a fully qualified path in cmd.exe

```
D:\> "D:\Apps\HelloWorld.exe"
Hello, World!
```

Example 7-2. Entering a fully qualified path in MSH

```
MSH D:\MshScripts> "D:\Apps\HelloWorld.exe"
D:\Apps\HelloWorld.exe
```

cmd.exe is running the program, whereas MSH is happy to echo back the string that it's just been given. This difference can be reconciled with the ampersand (&) syntax, which forces MSH to interpret a string as a command.

How Do I Do That?

MSH treats anything enclosed in quotation marks as a string. Even if it looks like a path, cmdlet name, alias, or function, MSH will not give material enclosed in quotation marks any special treatment.

Prefixing a string with the & character tells MSH that the string immediately following it is to be run as either an alias, cmdlet, function, script, or executable, following exactly the same execution rules we saw in Chapter 2:

```
MSH D:\MshScripts> & "D:\Apps\HelloWorld.exe"
Hello, World!
```

The string must contain only the command to be executed, and any options to the command should be supplied separately. Otherwise, MSH tries to find the whole thing—command, options, and all—which doesn't usually have the desired effect:

```
MSH D:\MshScripts> & "get-help new-object"
: 'get-help new-object' is not recognized as a Cmdlet, function, operable
program, or script file.
At line:1 char:2
+ &" <<<< get-help new-object"

MSH D:\MshScripts> & "get-help" new-object

NAME
    new-object

SYNOPSIS
    [-TypeName] type-name
                [[-Arguments] arguments]
                [-AssemblyName]
                [-FileName]
    ...
```

Many command-line tools use an *errorlevel* or *exit code* to indicate success, failure, or some additional status after the program has run. A common technique in *cmd.exe* batch file authoring involves a statement such as IF errorlevel 3 GOTO label, which allows a batch file to make a decision based on the outcome of an external program. This same information is available to MSH scripts by way of the $LASTEXITCODE global variable:

```
MSH D:\MshScripts> ping nonexistenthost
Ping request could not find host foo. Please check the name and try again.
MSH D:\MshScripts> $lastexitcode
1
MSH D:\MshScripts> ping 127.0.0.1

Pinging 127.0.0.1 with 32 bytes of data:
```

```
Reply from 127.0.0.1: bytes=32 time<1ms TTL=128
Reply from 127.0.0.1: bytes=32 time<1ms TTL=128
Reply from 127.0.0.1: bytes=32 time<1ms TTL=128
Reply from 127.0.0.1: bytes=32 time<1ms TTL=128

Ping statistics for 127.0.0.1:
    Packets: Sent = 4, Received = 4, Lost = 0 (0% loss),
Approximate round trip times in milli-seconds:
    Minimum = 0ms, Maximum = 0ms, Average = 0ms

MSH D:\MshScripts> $lastexitcode
0
```

What Just Happened?

Here we've seen one of the subtle yet significant differences between MSH and *cmd.exe*. For consistency, MSH treats all objects in a predictable manner. In the case of a filename, MSH is unable to distinguish whether the intent is to run an executable or just store a string that points to it. More information is needed (in the form of an &) to indicate to the shell that it should treat the string differently. It should come as no surprise that if Tab completion in MSH results in a quoted string (which will happen if there are spaces in the path or filename), the shell automatically prefixes it with &, and therefore ensures that the command shell tries to run the executable as expected.

Error and exit codes have been used for a long time as a medium for a command-line tool to pass on some information about its execution, and they are usually used to determine exactly what (if anything) went wrong. While it serves this purpose well enough, there is a limit to the amount of useful information that can be captured in a single number. With MSH, we generally find that cmdlets report information in the type and number of objects they return, leaving little need for an additional exit code. However, when interoperating with other command-line tools, the value of an exit code can be critical to further decision making. Because the $lastexitcode variable is updated with every external program that is run, make sure to check it immediately after running each external command when running several in sequence. Otherwise, you'll only be able to see the status of the last one. While MSH updates this variable automatically when an external command is run, MSH cmdlets and scripts can also modify it by a simple assignment, which can be useful for testing purposes.

What About...

How do I start a program associated with a file extension? In *cmd.exe*, typing the name of a nonexecutable file (for example, a Word document) has the same effect as double-clicking the file from Explorer—namely, its associated application is started and the document is loaded. The & symbol is used only for starting executable programs in MSH and does not offer the same behavior. Instead, the invoke-item cmdlet should be used on the file to emulate this behavior. invoke-item . is identical to the *cmd.exe* start . command. The get-command cmdlet can be used with a wildcard (get-command *) or partial wildcard (get-command *txt) to show a list of all possible invocations in the current environment.

Parse Text-Based Application Output

Many administrators find a handful of command-line tools invaluable in their day-to-day tasks. Using the & syntax, we've seen how simple it is to work these tools into newer MSH scripts, but that's only half of the challenge. What is to be done when these legacy tools generate output? *cmd.exe* batch files and most command-line utilities are still limited to generating textual output, but given the string manipulation functionality in MSH, that needn't be an obstacle.

How Do I Do That?

We'll focus on a commonly used tool for diagnosing network status and problems: ping. The ping tool ships with Windows and is used to send a series of ping packets to a destination to see whether the destination machine is reachable over the network. Let's see some typical output of the ping tool:

```
MSH D:\MshScripts> ping 127.0.0.1

Pinging 127.0.0.1 with 32 bytes of data:

Reply from 127.0.0.1: bytes=32 time<1ms TTL=128
Reply from 127.0.0.1: bytes=32 time<1ms TTL=128
Reply from 127.0.0.1: bytes=32 time<1ms TTL=128
Reply from 127.0.0.1: bytes=32 time<1ms TTL=128

Ping statistics for 127.0.0.1:
    Packets: Sent = 4, Received = 4, Lost = 0 (0% loss),
Approximate round trip times in milli-seconds:
    Minimum = 0ms, Maximum = 0ms, Average = 0ms
```

That output looks regular—a characteristic that makes it a good candidate for parsing. We'll start with a function called IsMachineUp, which will invoke ping and determine whether valid replies were received. This function calls *ping.exe*, collects each line of its output, filters to show only those rows containing the Reply text, and uses that to conclude whether the ping succeeded:

```
MSH D:\MshScripts> function IsMachineUp {
>>$lines = $(&"ping.exe" $args[0] | where {$_ -match "^Reply.*bytes=" })
>>($lines.Count -gt 0)
>>}
>>
MSH> IsMachineUp www.oreilly.com
True
MSH> IsMachineUp nonexistentmachine
False
```

We can take this one step further and actually convert the results into a more comfortable format for use inside MSH. The following function builds on the same idea as before, but this time uses some string manipulation to extract the interesting fields from the Reply lines:

```
MSH D:\MshScripts> function ping {
>>$lines = $(&"ping.exe" $args[0] | where {$_ -match "^Reply"})
>>foreach ($line in $lines)
>>{
>>   $parts=$line.Split(" ")
>>   $bytesPair=$parts[3].Split("=")
>>   $bytes=$bytesPair[1]
>>   $timePair=$parts[4].Split("=<")     # separated by < or =
>>   $time=$timePair[1].Replace("ms","")  # drop ms suffix
>>   $ttlPair=$parts[5].Split("=")
>>   $ttl=$ttlPair[1]
>>     1|select-object `
>>     @{expression = {$bytes}; name = "Bytes"},`
>>     @{expression = {$time}; name = "Time"},`
>>     @{expression = {$ttl}; name = "TTL"}
>>}
>>}
>>
MSH D:\MshScripts> ping www.oreilly.com
```

Bytes	Time	TTL
32	167	244
32	101	244
32	97	244
32	106	244

```
MSH D:\MshScripts> ping www.oreilly.com | measure-object -Property Time
-Average
```

```
Count     : 4
Average   : 112.75
Sum       :
Max       :
Min       :
Property  : Time
```

What Just Happened?

Before we dig into how this example works, let's take a step back and look at some of the consequences of this approach. Although we've successfully transformed the output of the ping command into a structured format that can be used elsewhere in the shell, we've undermined a few of the key principles that give MSH its flexibility. By choosing to parse the text-based output of a command, we've reduced the robustness of the solution. If the output of the ping command were to change its format in response to a network condition, the parsing rules we've assumed might become invalid.

With that caveat in mind, let's look at what just happened. In the first function, the goal is to capture the output of the ping command with a variable. Due to the presence of the where cmdlet, we can be confident that any lines matching the regular expression, which looks for successful ping responses, will be captured. To give a yes/no state of the availability, all that remains is to see whether any successful ping responses were found. Even just one reply line in the $lines array indicates that the remote machine returned something, so the function simply checks to see that one or more lines are present.

Taking it a step further, we can actually break up each line of the output into its constituent parts. Using the Split method of the string class inside a loop, each of the three data points—bytes returned, time taken, and TTL—can be separated into their own variables. select-object is then used to place a new object, with its fields populated, on the pipeline for each response. These objects become first-class citizens of MSH, and any of the familiar cmdlets can now be used on the data they hold.

What About...

...Extending the text-parsing approach to other command-line tools? Although anything that outputs text-based information can be parsed by an MSH script in this fashion, anything that relies heavily on string parsing will be brittle and prone to failure if the format changes in the future. Although ipconfig could be parsed to get a machine name, IP address, and MAC—or the net use output interpreted to understand mapped drives—all of this system configuration and state information is available via other channels, such as WMI and the .NET Framework Class Library.

Fill In the Blanks: Take Input from the Console

Early on, we looked at the distinction between interactive mode and script mode when using MSH: one expects line-by-line interaction at the console; the other can run in a completely automated fashion. However, some situations demand a middle ground in which a script is able to stop and wait for user input before processing continues.

Let's look at how to use the read-host cmdlet from within a script to gather input from the console.

How Do I Do That?

Starting with something very simple, let's look back at the "Hello, World" example. Example 7-3 contains a script that uses read-host to put information into a variable.

Example 7-3. HelloWorldInput.msh

```
$name=read-host "Name: "
write-host "Hello, $name!"
```

On running the script, the shell will wait indefinitely at the Name: prompt, waiting for some input:

```
MSH D:\MshScripts> .\HelloWorldInput.msh
Name: Andy
Hello, Andy!
```

Well-written scripts should be able to accommodate different types of invocation. A script that always blocks and waits for user input is not going to be effective running as a Scheduled Task, for example. When feasible, it is a good idea to support input from the command line and prompt only when none is found with a small modification to the original script, as shown in Example 7-4.

Example 7-4. HelloWorldInput2.msh

```
$name=$args[0]
if ($name -ne "")
{
    $name=read-host Name:
}

write-host "Hello, $name"
```

It's also worth mentioning that many cmdlets define *mandatory parameters*. By classifying parameters as mandatory, the cmdlet author is stating that the cmdlet cannot perform its task without having this information provided. An example of this is the get-content cmdlet, which requires at least one path from which to gather content. Calling the cmdlet with no parameters will generate an explicit prompt asking for the required information:

```
MSH D:\MshScripts> get-content

Cmdlet get-content at command pipeline position 1
Supply values for the following parameters:
(Type !? for Help.)
Path[0]:
```

Where Can I Learn More?

The built-in help for read-host provides usage information, additional detailed support for different prompt formats, and a mechanism for capturing sensitive information such as a password.

Untangle GOTO-Based Batch Files

Of all of the features of *cmd.exe*, two constructs have enabled batch file writers to create some very versatile scripts: the IF and GOTO statements. Although IF exists in MSH (albeit in a slightly different form), GOTO is notably absent. Thankfully, MSH functions, script flow control statements (if and switch), and script blocks are able to completely remove the need for the GOTO statement.

How Do I Do That?

The SHIFT command present in *cmd.exe* is used to shift all command-line arguments "up one." In other words, the first argument, %1, is dropped, %2 becomes %1, %3 becomes %2, and so on. Batch files can use this technique for processing each command-line argument in turn, as shown in Example 7-5.

Example 7-5. ProcessArguments.cmd

```
@ECHO OFF

:start
ECHO Processing %1

SHIFT
IF NOT "%1"=="" GOTO start
```

When given a set of options on the command line, this *cmd.exe* script will work through each in turn until none remains:

```
C:\> ProcessArguments.cmd a b c
Processing a
Processing b
Processing c
```

MSH offers a different solution, and it is something we've already discussed. Remember that to an MSH script, all command-line arguments are available in the $args special variable array. An MSH script (like that shown in Example 7-6) can simply use a foreach statement to walk through the list to achieve the same result.

Example 7-6. ProcessArguments.msh

```
foreach ($arg in $args)
{
    echo "Processing $arg"
}
```

Now, let's take a look at a batch file that copies one file to a destination but makes sure not to overwrite the target. The batch file in Example 7-7 requires two options to be present on the command line when the script is called; if either is empty, it displays a short usage guide and exits.

Example 7-7. CautiousCopy.cmd

```
@echo off

IF "%1"=="" GOTO usage
IF "%2"=="" GOTO usage

IF EXIST %2 GOTO nooverwrite

ECHO Executing copy %1 %2

GOTO end


:nooverwrite
ECHO Abort: Script will not overwrite %2
GOTO end


:usage
ECHO Usage information
ECHO.
ECHO   CautiousCopy.cmd file1 file2
GOTO end


:end
```

To recreate the same functionality in an MSH script, it's important to focus on the goals of the batch file rather than its current implementation. The new script in Example 7-8 will check that the options are present, check whether the target exists, and perform the copy, in that order.

Example 7-8. CautiousCopy.msh

```
if ($args.count -ne 2)
{
    echo "Usage"
    echo ""
    echo "   test.msh file1 file2"
    exit
}

if (test-path $args[1])
{
    echo "Abort: Script will not overwrite $($args[1])"
    exit
}

echo "Executing copy $($args[0]) $($args[1])"
```

Although there is little difference in the lengths of the two scripts, the MSH version is somewhat more sequential and easier to follow, meaning that future changes should be that much easier.

Another use of the GOTO statement allows a batch file to call itself in a recursive fashion as Example 7-9 does. In the first run, the batch file sets up the loop and then calls itself to process each entry. Some marker is used (the RECURSIVEMODE option in this case) to indicate to the script that it is calling itself and should behave differently.

Example 7-9. ProcessFiles.cmd

```
@echo off

IF "%1"=="RECURSIVEMODE" GOTO recursiveBlock
FOR %%f IN (*,*) DO @%0 RECURSIVEMODE %%f
GOTO end

:recursiveBlock
ECHO Processing %2

:end
```

In MSH, it is relatively rare for a script to call itself in this fashion. Indeed, although Example 7-9 does call itself recursively, it is only doing so to solve an iterative task. Problems like these are well-suited to a looping construct such as the foreach statement, which we've already discussed; Example 7-10 is a cleaner MSH script that has the same effect.

Example 7-10. ProcessFiles.msh

```
foreach ($file in $(get-childitem))
{
    echo "Processing $file"
}
```

What Just Happened?

By now, it should be apparent that, if nothing else, MSH can be used to write scripts that serve the same purpose as *cmd.exe* batch files. What's more, with some practice, the time taken to write and troubleshoot MSH scripts should decrease significantly.

Although the GOTO statement is an intuitive concept in a simple scripting language, its use can quickly lead to scripts that jump all over the place to do their work. They can become rigid such that even simple modifications or adjustments are nontrivial and troubleshooting problems can become expensive. In Examples 7-8, 7-9, and 7-10, the GOTO commands were a means to an end, providing some ability to either loop or control what happened next. In Chapter 3, we saw how these ideas are built into MSH, and it turns out that when the proper tools are available, there is often a more logical way to structure the script.

Of course, there are cases that fall outside of the examples covered here, and it might not be immediately obvious how to rework a batch file appropriately. Generally speaking, if several different places in the script call a GOTO to the same target, that target content should probably be wrapped up in an MSH function.

The removal of GOTO semantics is one of the more significant changes when facing a batch file to MSH migration, but now let's take a look at some of the similarities between the two shells.

Recap: Replacing Common Batch File Syntax

In this chapter, we've looked at several of the parallels between *cmd.exe* batch files and MSH scripts. It's safe to assume that anything that can be expressed in batch file syntax can be translated into an MSH script, but scripts cannot just be renamed and expected to run.

Table 7-1 is a quick reference that maps batch file syntax to MSH syntax. With more complex batch files, there may be a need to restructure their layout (especially if they're heavily dependent on GOTOs), but this should provide a good starting point.

Table 7-1. Batch file to MSH script cheat sheet

CMD.EXE batch file	MSH script
REM comment:: comment	# comment
PAUSE	read-host 'Press ENTER to continue'
CALL batchfile	& scriptfile
IF test command	if (test) { command }
IF NOT test command	if (!test) { command }
IF test command1 IF test command2	if (test) { command1; command2 }
IF EXIST path command	if (test-path path) { command }
SHIFT	$argPosition=0 # start of the script... $args[$argPosition++]
%* %1	$args $args[0]
FOR %%f IN (filespec) DO command	foreach ($f in $(get-childitem filespec)) { command }
IF ERRORLEVEL x command	if ($lastexitcode -eq x) { command }
GOTO label	See Untangle GOTO-based batch files
SET var=value	$env:var=value #environment variables $var=value #shell variables

Let's now turn our focus away from *cmd.exe* migration tasks and toward some everyday tasks that are well-suited to MSH scripts. We'll shift gears for the next few pages and cover a number of different commands, scripts, and functions without getting into too much detail.

Renaming Multiple Files at Once

To change the extensions of a folder of *.htm* files to *.html* files:

```
MSH D:\MshScripts> get-childitem *.htm | foreach-object { rename-item $_.
name $_.name.replace(".htm",".html") }
```

Instead of changing the extension, we can change part of the stem. For a folder containing *image1.gif, image2.gif*, etc., let's replace the "image" part with something more meaningful:

```
MSH D:\MshScripts> get-childitem image*.gif | foreach-object { rename-item
$_.name $_.name.replace("image", "inventory") }
```

Alternatively, we can change all filenames to be lowercase:

```
MSH D:\MshScripts> get-childitem | foreach-object { rename-item $_.name $_.
name.tolower() }
```

Match and Replace Content in a Text File

To change the content of a text file by replacing one string (e.g., "orig") with another (e.g., "update"):

```
MSH> get-content file.txt | foreach-object { $_ -replace "orig","update" } |
set-content file.txt
```

Filters can be well-suited for repetitive changes to pipeline objects, such as a sequence of files:

```
MSH D:\MshScripts> filter ReplaceInFile {
>>param($find,$replace)
>>get-content $_ | foreach-object { $_ -replace $find,$replace } | set-
content $_
>>}
>>
MSH D:\MshScripts> get-childitem *.msh | ReplaceInFile "Author:" "Written
by:"
```

List Recently Changed Files

To list any files that have been changed within the last day:

```
MSH D:\MshScripts> get-childitem –Recurse | where-object { $_.LastWriteTime
–gt (get-date).AddDays(-1) }
```

Counting Types of Files

Use group-object to categorize and count files by their type:

```
MSH D:\MshScripts> get-childitem | group-object {$_.Extension}
```

Find Out Which Command Is Being Run

Use a function to list all possible matches for an executable command in the order in which they are searched:

```
function which {
    param($search)

    # look for the search term in the possible invocation list
    get-command * | where-object { $_.Name -like $search }

    # look for the search term with possible extensions
    foreach ($ext in $($env:PATHEXT).Split(";"))
    {
        get-command * | where-object { $_.Name –like "$search$ext" }
    }
}
```

Downloading Content from the Web

The `System.Net.WebClient` class offers a `DownloadString` method that can be used to pull content directly from a URL. Because these examples are pulled from dynamic content on the Internet, the exact values in the output may change over time:

```
MSH D:\MshScripts> $wc = new-object System.Net.WebClient
MSH D:\MshScripts> $content = $wc.DownloadString("http://www.oreilly.com")
MSH D:\MshScripts> $content | measure-object -words -lines -characters


Lines            Words            Characters        Property
-----            -----            ----------        --------
1108             4554             54957
```

WebClient is not particular about the type of content it downloads. If a URL points to XML content, it is perfectly legitimate to cast the string to an XmlDocument and work with it from there:

```
MSH D:\MshScripts> $xml = [Xml]$wc.DownloadString("http://www.oreillynet.
com/rss/render/160.rss")
MSH D:\MshScripts> $xml.GetElementsByTagName("item") | format-table title


title
-----
Exchange Server Cookbook
ASP.NET 2.0: A Developer's Notebook
Knoppix Pocket Reference
Firefox Secrets: A Need-to-Know Guide
Mapping Hacks
Mac OS X Tiger Pocket Guide
Learning Unix for Mac OS X Tiger
Assembling Panoramic Photos: A Designer's Notebook
DHTML Utopia: Modern Web Design Using JavaScript and DOM
Toad Pocket Reference for Oracle, 2nd Edition
Mac OS X Tiger for Unix Geeks
```

Shorthand for Frequently Used Data

To generate a Windows-style domain and username combination:

```
MSH D:\MshScripts> function whoami { "$env:USERDOMAIN\$env:USERNAME" }
```

For quick access to the current time and other convenient instants:

```
MSH D:\MshScripts> alias now get-date
MSH D:\MshScripts> function yesterday { (get-date).AddDays(-1) }
MSH D:\MshScripts> function tomorrow { (get-date).AddDays(1) }
MSH D:\MshScripts> function lastweek { (get-date).AddWeeks(-1) }
```

For a quick report of the operating system and version from WMI:

```
MSH D:\MshScripts> function ver { $os = get-wmiobject Win32_OperatingSystem;
"$($os.Caption)`n$($os.CSDVersion)" }
```

Returning System Uptime

First, start with a function for converting WMI date formats into `DateTime` objects:

```
function parsewmidate {
    param($wmidate)

    $year = [int]$wmidate.substring(0, 4)
    $month = [int]$wmidate.substring(4,2)
    $day = [int]$wmidate.substring(6,2)
    $hour = [int]$wmidate.substring(8,2)
    $min = [int]$wmidate.substring(10,2)
    $sec = [int]$wmidate.substring(12,2)

    new-object DateTime $year,$month,$day,$hour,$min,$sec
}
```

Use the Win32_OperatingSystem WMI class to calculate uptime and time since last rebuild:

```
function uptime {
    $reboot = parsewmidate $(get-wmiobject Win32_OperatingSystem).
LastBootupTime
    new-timespan $reboot $(get-date)
}

function sinceRebuild {
{
    $rebuild = parsewmidate $(get-wmiobject Win32_OperatingSystem).
InstallDate
    new-timespan $rebuild $(get-date)
}
```

Simple UI Automation

Use the Windows Script Host object model to emulate physical interaction with an application by sending it keystrokes:

```
$wsh = new-object -ComObject "WScript.Shell"
$wsh.Run("calc")

start-sleep 1

if ($wsh.AppActivate("Calculator"))
{
  "Calc activated"

  $keystrokes="1","{+}","2","{+}","3","{=}"
  foreach ($key in $keystrokes)
```

```
{
  start-sleep 1
  "Sending $key"
  $wsh.SendKeys($key)
}

"Done"
}
```

The script introduces a small pause between keystrokes to ensure that the application is able to receive and process each in turn. To the application (Calculator, in this case), it appears as though the keystrokes are coming from a real user via the keyboard.

Colorize the Output of get-childitem

Use a filter to colorize the output of a file listing. Customize the coloring rules by modifying the hashtable or changing the logic in the filter to color by something different.

```
$colors=@{msh = "Red"; exe = "Green"; cmd = "Green"; directory = "Blue" }
$defaultColor = "Gray"

filter color-files {
    if ($_.Extension -ne "") { $ext = $_.Extension.Substring(1) }
    if ($_.Mode.StartsWith("d")) { $ext = "directory" }
    if ($colors.ContainsKey($ext)) { $color = $colors[$ext] }
    else { $color = $defaultColor }
    write-host -ForegroundColor $color $_
}
```

After dot sourcing the script, use it in the pipeline after get-childitem to bring color to the console:

```
MSH> get-childitem | color-files
```

Figure 7-1 shows the result.

What's Left?

MSH is a versatile and extensible environment and, as such, the list of these little script snippets could go on indefinitely. However, now it is time to take some of the examples we've covered here and head out into the world of MSH. Borrow whatever examples you like, discard what you don't need, and don't be afraid to build up script snippets and functions by experimentation (on a nonproduction system, of course!).

Good luck!

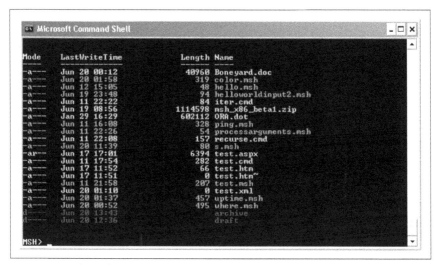

Figure 7-1. Colorized get-childitem output

Syntax and Grammar

This appendix covers the basic syntax and grammar rules of MSH and should be a useful reference while learning MSH. For an exhaustive list of the syntax and grammar intricacies, use the built-in help system (get-help).

Cmdlets

All cmdlets follow an enforced verb-noun naming convention of the form verb-noun. If a verb is omitted, the get- form of cmdlet is used.

Operators

Operators are used universally for setting, modifying, and comparing information as it passes around the shell.

Arithmetic

The arithmetic operators allow mathematical calculations within the shell. Table A-1 describes the available arithmetic operators and shows how they are used with numbers.

Table A-1. Arithmetic operators

Operator	Description	Example	Result
+	Add two numbers	8+2	10
-	Subtract one number from another	8-2	6
	Negate a number	-8	-8
*	Multiply two numbers	8*2	16
/	Divide one number by another	8/2	4
( )	Change calculation order and evaluate the enclosed first	(8-6)*2	4
%	Remainder of a division (modulus)	8%3	2

When multiple arithmetic operators are combined in a single expression, MSH follows a precedence sequence for evaluation. The unary - operator (negate a number) will always be evaluated first, followed by multiply (*), divide (/), remainder (%), add (+), and subtract (-). Parentheses ((expression)) can be used to override the default operator-evaluation order.

Some arithmetic operators are overloaded for other types. In particular, when strings are used, the add and multiply operators act differently, as shown in Table A-2.

Table A-2. Arithmetic operators on strings

Operator	Description	Example	Result
+	Concatenate two strings	"a"+"b"	"ab"
*	Repeat a string	"c"*6	"cccccc"

Assignment

Assignment operators are used for defining and updating variable values. Although most composite operations are designed for use on numbers, the += and *= operators can also be used on strings.

For the examples in Table A-3, assume that the variable $a has already been assigned a value of 8.

Table A-3. Assignment operators

Operator	Description	Example	Result
=	Set a variable	$a=1	$a is 1
+=	Add to a variable	$a+=3	$a is 11
-=	Subtract from a variable	$a-=2	$a is 6
*=	Multiply a variable	$a*=2	$a is 16
/=	Divide a variable	$a/=2	$a is 4
%=	Set a variable to the remainder of a division	$a%=3	$a is 2
++	Increment a number variable	$a++ ++$a	$a is 9, returns 8 $a is 9, returns 9
--	Decrement a number variable	$a-- --$a	$a is 7, returns 8 $a is 7, returns 7

Negation

Monad provides two versions of the unary logical not operator, as shown in Table A-4.

Table A-4. Unary logial not operators

Operator	Description
-not	Logical not
!	Logical not

General Comparison

Comparison operators are frequently used in evaluating test conditions for loops and flow-control statements (see Table A-5).

Table A-5. General comparison operators

Operator	Description
-eq	Equal to
-lt	Less than
-gt	Greater than
-le	Less than or equal to
-ge	Greater than or equal to
-ne	Not equal to
-and	Logical AND
-or	Logical OR

String Comparison

All of the general comparison operators listed in Table A-5 act in a case-insensitive fashion and can be used meaningfully on strings. Table A-6 lists a number of additional string-specific comparison operators.

Table A-6. String operators

Operator	Description
-ieq	Equal to (ignore case)
-ilt	Less than (ignore case)
-igt	Greater than (ignore case)
-ile	Less than or equal to (ignore case)
-ige	Greater than or equal to (ignore case)
-ine	Not equal to (ignore case)
-ceq	Equal to (case-sensitive)
-clt	Less than (case-sensitive)
-cgt	Greater than (case-sensitive)
-cle	Less than or equal to (case-sensitive)

Table A-6. String operators (continued)

Operator	Description
-cge	Greater than or equal to (case-sensitive)
-cne	Not equal to (case-sensitive)
-like	Compare strings by wildcard (ignore case)
-notlike	Compare strings by wildcard (ignore case)
-ilike	Compare strings by wildcard (ignore case)
-inotlike	Compare strings by wildcard (ignore case)
-clike	Compare strings by wildcard (case-sensitive)
-cnotlike	Compare strings by wildcard (case-sensitive)
-match	Compare strings using a regular expression
-notmatch	Compare strings using a regular expression
-imatch	Compare strings using a regular expression (ignore case)
-inotmatch	Compare strings using a regular expression (ignore case)
-cmatch	Compare strings using a regular expression (case-sensitive)
-cnotmatch	Compare strings using a regular expression (case-sensitive)

Array-Containment Operators

Instead of iterating through every element, use array-containment operators to easily determine whether a given array contains a specified element (see Table A-7).

Table A-7. Array containment operators

Operator	Description
-contains	Look for an element in an array
-icontains	Look for an element in an array (case-insensitive)
-ccontains	Look for an element in an array (case-sensitive)

Bitwise Operators

Bitwise operators are commonly used for comparing flags and bit masks (see Table A-8).

Table A-8. Bitwise operators

Operator	Description
-band	Bitwise AND
-bor	Bitwise OR
-bnot	Bitwise NOT

Data Types

MSH has a set of well-known data types that correspond to the basic types in the .NET Framework.

Numbers

Numbers can be represented as integers or double precision floating-point values. MSH will automatically convert a number to its appropriate integer or double format depending on the presence of a decimal point. Conversion between number formats can be achieved with the explicit casting syntax [ ]:

```
MSH> $a = 10           # $a is an int
MSH> $b = 3.14         # $b is a double
MSH> $c = 0x20         # $c is an int (value 32 decimal)
MSH> $d = [int]1.2     # $d is an int (value 1)
MSH> $e = [double]3e2  # $e is a double (value 300.0)
```

MSH also supports the K, M, and G suffixes on integers to represent the kilo, mega, and giga multipliers of 2^{10}, 2^{20}, and 2^{30}, respectively:

```
MSH> 2K
2048
MSH> 8M
8388608
MSH> 3G
3221225472
```

Strings

Strings can be defined either with single (') or double quotation marks ("). For a string in single quotes, the shell does no variable replacement and treats the string literally. For a string enclosed in double quotes, the shell performs variable expansion, trying to change any variable substrings into the values of the corresponding variables.

Arrays

An array can contain zero or more elements. Arrays are defined by separating the elements by commas. The empty array (one which is not null but contains no elements) is signified by @( ) notation.

All arrays allow their content to be retrieved by an indexer. Including a numerical index inside square brackets after an array will return a specific element or result in an out-of-range exception. Arrays also support the Count property, which indicates the number of elements present:

```
MSH> $arr=1,2,3
MSH> $arr[1]
2
MSH> $arr=$(get-process)
MSH> $arr.Count
48
```

Hashtables (Associative Arrays)

Hashtables are a special type of array that offers user-defined keys to identify their elements instead of a numerical index. Hashtables are defined by
separating key=value pairs with semicolons inside curly braces. The empty
hashtable is signified by the @{} notation.

Hashtables allow their content to be retrieved by the associative indexer
(user-defined key). Like arrays, the key is included in square brackets to
retrieve a corresponding value from a hashtable. Hashtables also include
two collections, Keys and Values, that contain the set of keys and values,
respectively:

```
MSH> $ht= @{zeus = "andy"; apollo = "jack"}
MSH> $ht["zeus"]
andy
MSH> $ht.Zeus
andy
MSH> $ht.Values
andy
jack
```

Automatic Variables

The shell defines a number of automatic variables that have special meaning
depending on their context within the shell (see Table A-9). See the help
about_automatic_variables page for an exhaustive list.

Table A-9. Automatic variables

Variable	Value
$?	Success/fail status of the previous operation
$_	Contains the current pipeline object
$^	Contains the first token of the last line received by the shell
$$	Contains the last token of the last line received by the shell
$args	Contains the set of command-line options passed to a function, filter, or script after any named parameters are consumed
$input	Contains an enumerator of objects entering a function from the pipeline

Table A-9. Automatic variables (continued)

Variable	Value
$lastexitcode	The error level return from the last external command
$error	Array of errors (first element is the most recent)
$null	Null
$true	Boolean true value
$false	Boolean false value

Global Variables

A set of global variables is defined by the shell at startup for convenience (see Table A-10).

Table A-10. Default global variables

Variable	Value
$home	User's home directory
$host	Information about the MSH runtime
$mshhome	Path of currently running *msh.exe*
$pid	Process ID of current *msh.exe* process
$pwd	Current working directory

Preference Variables

MSH uses several variables to hold the default values to be used when a ubiquitous parameter is not explicitly set on a cmdlet. For cmdlets that respect the ubiquitous parameters, the values of these variables will be used unless explicitly overridden on invocation. See Table A-11 for a list of preference variables.

Table A-11. Preference variables

Variable	Meaning
$ConfirmPreference	Defines the default –Confirm setting
$DebugPreference	Defines the default –Debug setting
$ErrorActionPreference	Defines the default –ErrorAction setting
$VerbosePreference	Defines the default –Verbose setting
$WhatIfPreference	Defines the default –WhatIf setting

Execution Flow

MSH offers two mechanisms for controlling the flow of script execution: the if statement and the switch statement.

if Statement

```
if (<test 1>) { <block 1> }
elseif (<test2>) { <block 2> }
...
else { <block 3> }
```

As soon as one of the tests evaluates to true, the corresponding block is executed and no other tests are performed. The elseif and else parts of the statement are optional.

switch Statement

```
switch (<expression>)
{
    <value> { <block 1> }            # case 1
    {<test>} { <block 2> }           # case 2
    default { <block 3> }            # case 3
}
```

In case 1, MSH performs a test on the expression and value and, if they are equal, executes the first block. In case 2, MSH evaluates the test (in which $_ is used for the value of <expression>), and if the test evaluates to true, the second block is run. There may be many instances of these two cases, each using a different value or test. The default case (case 3) may only occur once and its associated block is run only if none of the other cases results in a match. Switch statements do not terminate after a match is made; instead, the blocks associated with all matching tests are run.

Loops

While looping is a general concept, MSH offers three specific mechanisms for performing iterative tasks: the while loop, the for loop, and the foreach loop.

while Loop

```
while (<condition>)
{ <block> }
```

The while loop is the simplest of loops and will repeatedly execute a block until a condition no longer holds true. The script block must at some point break the condition or there must be an external expectation that the condition will cease to hold at some point in the future; otherwise, the loop will continue indefinitely.

for Loop

```
for (<initialization>; <condition>; <repeat command>)
{ <block> }
```

The for loop gives complete control of the start, middle, and end of the loop. Like while, the condition is tested before each run, and the block is executed if a condition holds true. Additionally, a for statement can include an initialization statement that is run once (for example, to set a counter to zero). The repeat command is also optional (but recommended!) and is executed after each run through the block.

foreach Loop

```
foreach (<element> in <elements>)
{ <block> }
```

The foreach loop is well suited to processes in a collection such as an array or a sequence of objects emitted from a cmdlet. The block is executed once for each object in the elements list. During each invocation, the variable named in the <element> part is populated with the current object.

The foreach language element (described here) is different than the foreach-object cmdlet (which is also aliased as foreach). The foreach-object cmdlet is designed for pipeline use and does not take a (<element> in <elements>) term.

Functions and Filters

Functions and filters are defined with the same syntax and differ only in the way in which they operate.

Functions

```
function <functionname>
{
    param($a = 3, $b = "sample")
    <block>
}
```

Functions can output objects into the pipeline by simply including them in the block body or explicitly using return.

Arguments passed to a function on the command line will be matched against variables defined by the param section, and the remainder will be available in the $args special array. If these arguments are included in a pipeline, all earlier pipeline stages will complete before the function is run, at which point any pipeline content will be available in the $input special array.

Filters

```
filter <filtername>
{
    param($a = 3, $b = "sample")
    <block>
}
```

Like functions, filters output objects into the pipeline either by simply including the object in the block body or via the use of return. Again, if present, arguments are filled into the appropriate variables defined by the param statement, with the remainder ending up in the $args special argument. A filter is only used in a pipeline setting and will be invoked for every object. For each invocation, the special variable $_ will contain the pipeline object to process.

Resolution Order

When interpreting a script, MSH uses the following ordering:

- Alias
- Function/filter
- Cmdlet
- Files with extensions defined by $env:PATHEXT in $env:PATH

Standard Cmdlets, Functions, and Aliases

The tables that follow list the standard cmdlets, functions, and aliases that are made available as part of a standard MSH installation. This reference is not a replacement for the information available through get-help. Rather, it is intended to provide an overview and brief description of the available cmdlets.

Standard Cmdlets

The sections that follow have been separated into groups based on the subject of the cmdlet. Remember that get-help supports wildcard syntax, so it is easy to find commands related to a specific cmdlet. For example, to find commands related to get-object, type get-help *-object.

System

Cmdlet	Description
get-command	Returns a list of available commands
invoke-command	Invokes the command specified by the given string (as if it were typed at the prompt)
get-host	Returns information about the MSH host
get-culture	Returns information about the regional settings of the host (as defined in the Regional Settings of the Control Panel)
get-help	Provides built-in help functionality
get-uiculture	Returns information about the regional settings of the host as defined by the selected language on a multi-language operating system

Objects

Cmdlet	Description
foreach-object	Applies script blocks to each object in the pipeline
where-object	Filters the input from the pipeline, allowing operation on only certain objects
get-member	Enumerates properties, methods, type info, and property sets of the objects given to it
new-object	Instantiates a new .NET or COM object
select-object	Selects objects based on parameters set in the cmdlet command string
group-object	Collects objects together based on a common property value
sort-object	Arranges objects in sequence based on a property value

History

Cmdlet	Description
get-history	Returns a list of session history
invoke-history	Invokes an entry from the session history
add-history	Adds an entry to the session history

Cmdlet Providers

Cmdlet	Description
new-drive	Creates a new drive associated with a cmdlet provider
get-provider	Returns a list of all registered cmdlet providers and the drives associated with each provider

Drives

Cmdlet	Description
remove-drive	Removes a drive association from a cmdlet provider
get-drive	Returns a list of all drives registered with cmdlet providers

Paths and locations

Cmdlet	Description
combine-path	Combines path elements into a single path
convert-path	Converts the path to the item given from an MSH path to a provider path
parse-path	Given an MSH path(s), streams a string with the qualifier, parent path, or leaf item

Cmdlet	Description
test-path	Returns true if the path exists, otherwise returns false
resolve-path	Resolves the wildcards in a path
get-location	Displays the current location
set-location	Sets the current working location to a specified location
push-location	Pushes a location to the stack
pop-location	Changes the current working location to the location specified by the last entry pushed onto the stack

Properties

Cmdlet	Description
get-property	Retrieves the properties of an object
move-property	Moves a property from one location to another
copy-property	Copies a property between locations or namespaces
clear-property	Removes the property value from a property
new-property	Sets a new property of an item at a location
remove-property	Removes a property and its value from the location
rename-property	Renames a property at its location
set-property	Sets a property at the specified location to a specified value

Items

Cmdlet	Description
get-item	Returns an object that represents an item in a namespace
new-item	Creates a new item in a namespace
set-item	Sets the value of a pathname within a provider to the specified value
remove-item	Deletes an item from a provider
move-item	Transfers an item from one location to another, removing the original
rename-item	Changes the name of an existing item
copy-item	Copies an item from one location to another, leaving the original intact
clear-item	Removes the content of an item
invoke-item	Invokes an executable or opens a file
get-childitem	Retrieves the child items of the specified location(s) in a drive
get-acl	Gets the access control list (ACL) associated with a file or item
set-acl	Sets the security ACL for an item or items

Content

Cmdlet	Description
add-content	Appends content to a file or creates a file if one does not exist
clear-content	Removes content from a file while leaving the file intact
get-content	Returns the content of a file as a sequence of lines
set-content	Replaces the content of a file with new content

Operating System Components

Cmdlet	Description
get-eventlog	Returns a list of event log entries from a specified event log
get-wmiobject	Returns data from WMI
get-process	Returns a list of running system processes
stop-process	Terminates a running process
get-service	Returns a list of registered system services
stop-service	Terminates a running system service
start-service	Starts a stopped system service
suspend-service	Pauses a running system service
resume-service	Reactivates a paused system service
restart-service	Stops then restarts a system service
set-service	Configures the properties of a registered system service
new-service	Registers a new system service

Output Formatters

Cmdlet	Description
format-list	Formats objects as a list of their properties displayed vertically
format-table	Formats objects as a tabulated list (one line per object)
format-wide	Formats objects as a tabulated list (several objects per line)
out-null	Drops all output
out-default	Sends output to the host; not called from the command line
out-host	Sends output to the host
out-file	Sends output to a file
out-printer	Sends output to a printer
out-string	Sends output to a string
import-csv	Generates a sequence of objects from a comma-separated variable file
export-csv	Writes a sequence of objects to a file in comma-separated form

Aliases

Cmdlet	Description
set-alias	Maps an alias to a command
get-alias	Returns a list of all defined aliases
new-alias	Creates a new alias
export-alias	Outputs the system alias table in CSV format
import-alias	Updates the system alias table from a CSV file

Miscellaneous

Cmdlet	Description
get-date	Returns the current date and time
set-date	Updates the system date and time
match-string	Searches through a string or file(s) for a pattern
measure-object	Calculates arithmetical statistics on specific properties of pipeline objects
new-timespan	Calculates the time difference between two specified DateTime objects
start-sleep	Pauses processing for a specified number of seconds or milliseconds

Variables

Cmdlet	Description
get-variable	Returns the value of a variable
new-variable	Creates a new variable with a specified name and value
set-variable	Updates or creates a new variable with a specified name and value; useful at the end of a pipeline for storing objects into a variable for later use
remove-variable	Removes a variable definition from the variable list
clear-variable	Removes the value of a variable but leaves its definition in place (i.e., sets its value to null)

Input/Output

Cmdlet	Description
write-host	Writes an object to the hosting environment (usually the console)
write-progress	Writes to the host's progress display channel
write-object	Writes an object to the pipeline
write-debug	Writes an object into the debug pipeline

Cmdlet	Description
write-verbose	Writes an object to the host's verbose display channel; output may or may not be shown depending on the host settings
write-error	Writes an object to the error pipeline
read-host	Reads data from the hosting environment (usually the console)

Security

Cmdlet	Description
get-pfxcertificate	Returns an X509Certificate from a file
get-credential	Generates a credential by asking an interactive user to provide a password
get-authenticodesignature	Returns the Authenticode signature from a file
set-authenticodesignature	Updates the Authenticode signature on a file
new-securestring	Creates a string that can be used to safely store and work with sensitive information (e.g., passwords)
export-securestring	Converts a secure string into an encrypted representation in a regular string
import-securestring	Converts an encrypted string back into a secure string

Debugging

Cmdlet	Description
set-mshdebug	Enables/disables debugging and execution trace support
trace-expression	Enables tracing for a specified expression or command

Standard Functions

Several frequently used functions are defined in the standard shell.

Function	Description
clear-host	Clears the console
more	Displays output one screen at a time
help, man	Displays paged output of get-help
mkdir, md	Creates a new directory
A:...Z:	Sets current location to the relevant drive letter

Aliases

The standard set of aliases recreates the familiar behavior of the other command-line shells and ensures a consistent baseline experience for any MSH shell. Each alias maps to a standard cmdlet or defined function.

Note that some of these aliases (e.g., sc) may hide certain other applications present on your system. To run an external program, call it with its file extension (e.g., sc.exe) to make the distinction.

Some of the new aliases for commonly used commands are identified in bold.

Alias	Cmdlet
ac	add-content
clc	clear-content
cli	clear-item
clp	clear-property
clv	clear-variable
cpi	**copy-item**
cpp	copy-property
cvpa	convert-path
epal	export-alias
epcsv	export-csv
fc	format-custom
fl	**format-list**
foreach	**foreach-object**
ft	**format-table**
fw	format-wide
gal	get-alias
gc	**get-content**
gci	**get-childitem**
gcm	get-command
gdr	get-drive
ghy	get-history
gi	get-item
gl	get-location
gm	**get-member**
gp	get-property
gps	**get-process**

Alias	Cmdlet
group	**group-object**
gsv	get-service
gu	get-unique
gv	get-variable
ic	invoke-command
ihy	invoke-history
ii	**invoke-item**
ipal	import-alias
ipcsv	import-csv
mi	**move-item**
mp	move-property
nal	new-alias
ndr	new-drive
ni	new-item
nv	new-variable
oh	out-host
rdr	remove-drive
ri	**remove-item**
rni	**rename-item**
rnp	rename-property
rp	remove-property
rv	remove-variable
rvpa	resolve-path
sal	set-alias
sasv	start-service
sc	**set-content**
select	**select-object**
si	set-item
sl	**set-location**
sleep	Start-Sleep
sort	**sort-object**
sp	set-property
spps	stop-process
spsv	stop-service
sv	set-variable
where	**where-object**
cat	get-content

Alias	Cmdlet
cd	set-location
chdir	set-location
clear	clear-host
cls	clear-host
copy	copy-item
cp	copy-item
del	remove-item
dir	get-childitem
echo	write-object
erase	remove-item
h	get-history
history	get-history
kill	stop-process
lp	out-printer
ls	get-childitem
mount	new-drive
move	move-item
mv	move-item
popd	pop-location
ps	get-process
pushd	push-location
pwd	get-location
r	invoke-history
rd	remove-item
ren	rename-item
rm	remove-item
rmdir	remove-item
set	set-variable
type	get-content

Index

Symbols

& (ampersand), invoking commands with, 138–141

* (asterisk)
  quantifier in regular expressions, 90
  wildcard character, 86

^ (caret), special character in regular expressions, 88, 90, 93

$ (dollar sign)
  identifying variables with, 49, 83
  special character in regular expressions, 88, 90, 93

= (equals sign) assignment operator, 50

` (escape character), 32

`" escape sequence, 84

`$ escape sequence, 84

`' escape sequence, 84

`` escape sequence, 84

` (grave accent character), 83–85

- (hyphen character), defining ranges using, 87

$_ notation, 15

-? option, 39

. (period), special character in regular expressions, 90

+ (plus sign), quantifier in regular expressions, 90

(pound) symbol for comments, 25

? (question mark)
  quantifier in regular expressions, 90
  wildcard character, 86

$$ variable, 160

$? variable, 160

$^ variable, 160

$_ variable, 54, 60, 72, 73, 160, 164

| (vertical bar)
  creating pipelines with (see pipelines)
  specifying alternates in regular expressions, 89

*= compound assignment operator, 52

+= compound assignment operator, 52

-= compound assignment operator, 52

/= compound assignment operator, 52

:: (double colon) for static methods/properties, 114, 116

() (parentheses)
  grouping regular expressions, 89
  using to nest quotation marks, 83

{ } (curly braces), quantifier in regular expressions, 90

[ ] (square brackets)
  .NET Framework references, 110
  wildcard characters, 87

@( ) syntax (empty arrays), 53, 159

@{ } syntax (empty hashtables), 53, 160

`0 escape sequence, 84

We'd like to hear your suggestions for improving our indexes. Send email to *index@oreilly.com*.

A

`a escape sequence, 85
about_Comparison_Operators
    keyword, 60
ac alias, 171
ACLs (Access Control Lists), 132–137
ActiveX controls, 117
AddAuditRule method, 136
add-content cmdlet, 168
add-history cmdlet, 166
AddHours method, 122
add-integers function, 70
aliases
    functions and, 67
    multiple, pointing at same
        cmdlet, 30
    saving keystrokes with, 26–30
    standard set of, 171–173
aliases for commands, 6
ampersand (&), invoking commands
    with, 138–141
-and comparison operator, 57, 157
application logs, 119
applications, configuring with registry
    provider, 10
$args special variable, 68, 160, 164
$args special variable array, 146
arithmetic operators, syntax/grammar
    of, 155
arrays, 52
    de-duping, 104
    empty, 53, 159
    syntax/grammar of, 159
    variables and, 49
assignment by reference, 51, 54
assignment by value, 51, 53
assignment operators
    basic, 50
    compound, 52
    syntax/grammar of, 156
associative arrays (see hashtables)
audit rules, creating, 134, 136
AuditRuleFactory method, 136
automatic expansion of collections, 47
automatic type conversion, 110–113
automatic variables, syntax/grammar
    of, 160
average size of files in a directory,
    calculating, 101

B

`b escape sequence, 85
\b, special character in regular
    expressions, 90
background processes,
    auditing, 124–128
backquote/backtick (`), 83–85
-band bitwise operator, 158
batch file syntax, mapping to MSH
    syntax, 148
batch files, GOTO-based,
    untangling, 145–148
BIOS, output of get-wmiobject for, 130
bitwise operators, syntax/grammar
    of, 158
-bnot bitwise operator, 158
-bor bitwise operator, 158
break keyword, 65
built-in aliases, 29, 171
by-reference assignment, 51, 54
by-value assignment, 51, 53

C

cacls.exe tool, 132–137
calculated columns, 17
calling methods of .NET Class
    Library, 114–116
casting values into types explicitly, 111,
    113
cat alias, 172
cat command, 105
categorizing types of files, 150
-ccontains operator, 158
cd alias, 173
-ceq comparison operator, 157
-cge comparison operator, 158
-cgt comparison operator, 157
-characters option
    (measure-object), 105
chdir alias, 173
child scope and parent scope, 79–81
Class Library in .NET Framework, 40
Class Library (.NET), calling methods
    of, 114–116
classes and objects in .NET
    Framework, 41, 110
clc alias, 171
-cle comparison operator, 157

DirectoryInfo object, 62
DOSKEY.EXE, 31
   keystrokes, list of, 33
dot notation
   accessing levels of XML files, 109
   expressing properties of objects
       using, 48, 114
dot sourcing script files, 26, 79
double quotes and single quotes, 82–84
down arrows, navigating through history
       buffer, 31
downloading MSH from Web, 3
DownloadString method, 151
drives, installed by MSH, 8
duplicate lines from text files,
       removing, 104

E

echo alias, 173
else statement, 56
elseif statement, 56, 58
empty arrays, 53, 159
EntryType property, 121
enumerations, 112
environment, customizing your, 34–36
epal alias, 171
epcsv alias, 171
-eq comparison operator, 15, 58, 91,
       157
erase alias, 173
$error array, 95
error codes, 139
error handling in MSH, 94–100
$error special variable, 161
-ErrorAction option, 97–100
$ErrorActionPreference global
       variable, 100
$ErrorActionPreference variable, 161
escape characters, 82–85
escape sequences, commonly used, 84
event logs, monitoring, 119–124
Event Viewer tool (eventvwr.exe), 119,
       124
EventLog class, 123
Exclude parameter, 5
execution order in MSH, 164
exit codes, 139
-Expand option, 46
explicit casts, overriding type conversion
       rules using, 111, 113

export-alias cmdlet, 169
export-csv cmdlet, 107, 110, 131, 168
export-securestring cmdlet, 170

F

`f escape sequence, 85
FailureAudit property, 121
$false special variable, 161
fc alias, 171
file permissions, managing, 132–137
FileInfo objects, 73
files (multiple), renaming, 149
filtering
   by date ranges, 123
   records in event logs, 121
   unique objects, 103
filters in MSH, 71–75
   colorizing output of file listings, 153
   syntax/grammar of, 164
-first option (select-object), 102
fl alias, 171
flags and enumerations, 112
flow control
   syntax/grammar of, 162
   using comparisons, 55–60
folder names, assigning permissions
       based on, 133
for statement, 63
   syntax/grammar of, 163
foreach alias, 171
foreach statement, 63–65
   import-csv cmdlet and, 108
   syntax/grammar of, 163
foreach-object cmdlet, 65, 166
-ForEachObject option, 46
format-list cmdlet, 17, 20, 131, 168
format-table cmdlet, 18–21, 121, 168
formatting cmdlets, 16
formatting strings, 65
format-wide cmdlet, 20, 168
ft alias, 171
fully qualified classes, 110
function keys and history buffers, 31
functions
   capturing reusable behavior
       in, 66–71
   controlling access to, 76–81
   frequently used, 170
   syntax/grammar of, 164
fw alias, 171

G

gal alias, 171
gc alias, 171
gci alias, 171
gcm alias, 171
gdr alias, 171
-ge comparison operator, 157
get-acl cmdlet, 132–137, 167
get-alias cmdlet, 27, 30, 51, 169
get-authenticodesignature cmdlet, 25,
    170
get-childitem cmdlet, 37, 54, 69, 167
    scoping and, 81
    wildcards and, 86–88
get-command cmdlet, 7, 21, 30, 141,
    165
    alias for, 171
get-content cmdlet, 74, 104–106, 145,
    168
get-credential cmdlet, 170
get-culture cmdlet, 165
get-date cmdlet, 25, 169
get-drive cmdlet, 11, 166
get-eventlog cmdlet, 120–124, 168
get-help cmdlet, 7, 16, 165
get-history cmdlet, 31–34, 166
get-host cmdlet, 165
get-item cmdlet, 167
get-location cmdlet, 167
get-member cmdlet, 42, 46–48, 136,
    166
get-pfxcertificate cmdlet, 170
get-process cmdlet, 4–7, 13–20, 42–47,
    51, 67, 168
    aliases for, 30
    filtering output of, 23
get-ProcessByHandles function, 70
get-properties cmdlet, 68
get-property cmdlet, 10, 167
get-provider cmdlet, 11, 166
get-service cmdlet, 125–128, 132, 168
get-uiculture cmdlet, 165
get-variable cmdlet, 169
get-wmiobject cmdlet, 128–132, 168
ghy alias, 171
gi alias, 171
gl alias, 171
global: prefix, 78

global scope, 77, 80
global variables, 52
global variables, syntax/grammar
    of, 161
gm alias, 171
GOTO commands, 55
GOTO-based batch files,
    untangling, 145–148
gp alias, 171
gps alias, 171
grave accent character (`), 83–85
group alias, 172
GroupBy parameter, 18
grouping, combining with default
    formatter, 20
group-object cmdlet, 14, 150, 166
gsv alias, 172
-gt comparison operator, 15, 58, 157
gu alias, 172
gv alias, 172

H

h alias, 173
handling errors in MSH, 94–100
Hansen, Kenneth, x
hashtables, 50, 53
    format-table cmdlet and, 20
    removing elements from, 55
    syntax/grammar of, 160
head function, 104
help function, 170
help system for MSH, 7
here strings, 85
history alias, 173
history buffers, 31–34
    increasing size of, 33
HistoryInfo objects, 31
hives, 8–10
HKEY_CURRENT_USER (HKCU), 8
HKEY_LOCAL_MACHINE (HKLM), 8
$home global variable, 161
$host global variable, 161

I

ic alias, 172
-icontains operator, 158
Id property, 47
-ieq comparison operator, 157

if statement, 56–58
   syntax/grammar of, 162
   using within loops, 65
-ige comparison operator, 157
-igt comparison operator, 157
ihy alias, 172
ii alias, 172
-ile comparison operator, 157
-ilike comparison operator, 158
-ilt comparison operator, 157
-imatch comparison operator, 158
import-alias cmdlet, 169
import-csv cmdlet, 108, 110, 137, 168
import-securestring cmdlet, 170
incompatible types, comparing, 60
-ine comparison operator, 157
Information property, 121
-inotlike comparison operator, 158
-inotmatch comparison operator, 158
input from consoles, gathering, using
   read-host cmdlet, 144
$input special variable, 68, 70, 160
-InputObject option, 47
Inquire (ErrorAction value), 99
installing MSH, 3
instantiating COM objects, 117–118
interactive mode, entering commands
   in, 31–34
invoke-command cmdlet, 165
invoke-history cmdlet, 32, 166
invoke-item cmdlet, 141, 167
InvokeMethod method, 132
ipal alias, 172
ipcsv alias, 172
IsMachineUp function, 142

K

keystrokes, saving, with aliases, 26–30
keystrokes, sending to applications, 152
kill alias, 173

L

-last option (select-object), 102
$LastExitCode variable, 139, 161
-le comparison operator, 157
legacy tools, using in pipelines, 15
lfFaceName key, 10
libraries of scripts, creating, 22

-like comparison operator, 91–94, 158
-lines option (measure-object), 105
listing recently changed files, 150
literal comparisons, 59
literal strings, represented by single
   quotes, 82
local: prefix, 78
local scope, 77, 80
lookup tables for storing alias
   mappings, 28
loops, 61–66
   syntax/grammar of, 162
lp alias, 173
ls alias, 173
-lt comparison operator, 15, 58, 157

M

man function, 170
managed code and .NET
   Framework, 40
mandatory parameters, 145
mapping batch file syntax to MSH
   syntax, 148
mappings for aliases, 26–30
Mastering Regular Expressions, 89
-match comparison operator, 92–94,
   158
matching content in text files, 150
matching with wildcards, 86–88
   vs. regular expressions, 92–94
match-string cmdlet, 169
$MaximumHistoryCount variable, 33
md function, 170
measure-object cmdlet, 103–105, 169
MemberType parameter, 42, 46, 68
method overloading, 114–116
methods and classes, 41
mi alias, 172
mkdir function, 170
Modules property, 45
MonadLog event logs, 120
more command, 106
more function, 170
mount alias, 173
move alias, 173
move-item cmdlet, 167
move-property cmdlet, 167
mp alias, 172

Payette, Bruce, x
permissions (file), managing, 132–137
$pid global variable, 161
ping tool, 141–143
pipeline elements, transferring
        structured data between, 1, 5
pipelines
    creating, to pass information, 12–16
    filtering unique objects, 103
    functions in, 70
    transforming objects when passing
        through, 71–75
    ubiquitous parameters and, 36–39
    using scripts in, 23–25
popd alias, 173
pop-location cmdlet, 167
"prayer-based parsing", 1
precedence sequence for evaluating
        arithmetic operators, 156
preference variables, syntax/grammar
        of, 161
private scope, 80
Process class, 42
process lists
    combining cmdlets to produce, 6
    inspecting, 4
    pipelining cmdlets together, 13–14
    using scripts with, 23–25
Process objects, formatting, 17
ProcessModule objects, 47
ProcessName parameter, 14
ProcessName property, 47
ProcessThread objects, properties of, 47
profile.msh file, 34
profiles, customizing shells with, 34–36
prompt function, 36
properties, 41
    accessing, 44
    of objects, expressing using dot
        notation, 48, 114
-Property option (measure-object), 103
provider model, using to access registry
        like filesystem, 7–12
ps alias, 173
pushd alias, 173
push-location cmdlet, 167
pwd alias, 173
$pwd global variable, 161

Q

quantifiers used in regular
        expressions, 90
quoting rules in MSH, 82–84

R

r alias, 173
`r escape sequence, 85
rd alias, 173
rdr alias, 172
read-host cmdlet, 144, 170
records in event logs, limiting number
        returned, 120
RECURSIVEMODE option, 147
reference types, 51, 54
registry
    accessing like a filesystem, 7–12
    web site for more information, 11
Registry Editor tool (regedit.exe), 9
regular expressions, 89–94
remove-drive cmdlet, 166
remove-item cmdlet, 37, 167
remove-property cmdlet, 167
remove-variable cmdlet, 169
ren alias, 173
rename-item cmdlet, 167
rename-property cmdlet, 167
renaming multiple files, 149
repetitive work, using loops for, 61–66
replacing content in text files, 150
resolve-path cmdlet, 167
restart-service cmdlet, 127, 168
resume-service cmdlet, 168
ri alias, 172
rich tab completion on command
        line, 33
rm alias, 173
rmdir alias, 173
rni alias, 172
rnp alias, 172
rp alias, 172
rv alias, 172
rvpa alias, 172

S

About the Author

Andy Oakley is a graduate of Jesus College, Cambridge, England with a degree in computer science. Currently, as a lead program manager at Microsoft, he is building the new publishing system for MSDN that hosts the hundreds of thousands of pages of developer documentation published by Microsoft.

Colophon

Our look is the result of reader comments, our own experimentation, and feedback from distribution channels. Distinctive covers complement our distinctive approach to technical topics, breathing personality and life into potentially dry subjects.

The animal on the cover of *Monad* is the common toad (*Bufo vulgaris*), a familiar European species. There are over 200 known species under the genus *Bufo*, all of which secrete poisonous fluid from their skin. These secretions are often highly toxic to animals when ingested, and they can irritate human skin upon contact.

Bufos are fairly large-size toads, normally reaching between six and eight inches in length. They enjoy warm and wet environments and are found virtually everywhere in the world except the North and South Poles, preferring the tropics but settling for ponds, canals, and moist backyards. Toads are cold-blooded and usually nocturnal. They hibernate during the cold parts of the year.

All toads breathe through their skin and have superb hearing and eyesight. Toads are especially perceptive of movement, which is why they don't eat things that are already dead. Unlike frogs, most toads only leap when they are in danger; however, the common American toad leaps much more often than the European species. Toads eat a lot. One toad can eat 100 flies in 10 minutes using its long, sticky, lightning-quick tongue. Toad tongues are so fast that they cannot be followed by the human eye. This characteristic, among others, led primitive peoples to believe that toads were supernatural creatures. The modern belief that people can get warts from toads is likewise due to superstition rather than science.

Toads appear in cultural history as early as 2000 B.C.E. Because the toad's lifecycle is such that it is born in the springtime—which is the rainy season in most parts of the world—toads were associated with sexuality, fertility, and rain. Peruvian Indians worshipped the "Toad Mother," and ancient

Tanini peoples from Bolivia portrayed their "Earth Mother" as a monstrous toad. It also has been documented that the Olmecs consumed common toads for hallucinogenic purposes; the Mayans used a drink called chicha in their rituals, made of sugar fermented with a live toad and toad poisons. (O'Reilly advises against ever doing this.)

Marlowe Shaeffer was the production editor for *Monad*. Annette Pagliaro was the copyeditor. Lydia Onofrei proofread the book. Adam Witwer and Claire Cloutier provided quality control. Judy Hoer wrote the index. Loranah Dimant provided production assistance.

Karen Montgomery designed the cover of this book, based on a series design by Edie Freedman. The cover image is from *Wood's Natural History: Comprising Mammals, Birds, Reptiles and Fishes*. Karen Montgomery produced the cover layout with Adobe InDesign CS using Adobe's ITC Garamond font.

David Futato designed the interior layout. This book was converted by Keith Fahlgren to FrameMaker 5.5.6 with a format conversion tool created by Erik Ray, Jason McIntosh, Neil Walls, and Mike Sierra that uses Perl and XML technologies. The text font is Linotype Birka; the heading font is Adobe Myriad Condensed; and the code font is LucasFont's TheSans Mono Condensed. The illustrations that appear in the book were produced by Robert Romano, Jessamyn Read, and Lesley Borash using Macromedia Free-Hand MX and Adobe Photoshop CS. The tip and warning icons were drawn by Christopher Bing. This colophon was written by Lydia Onofrei.

9 780596 100094